WORKBOOK

English 3 Explorer

Jane Bailey
with Helen Stephenson

NATIONAL GEOGRAPHIC LEARNING | CENGAGE Learning

Australia • Brazil • Japan • Korea • Mexico • Singapore • Spain • United Kingdom • United States

English Explorer Workbook 3
Jane Bailey with Helen Stephenson

Publisher: Jason Mann

Adaptations Manager: Alistair Baxter

Assistant Editor: Manuela Barros

Senior Marketing Manager: Ruth McAleavey

Senior Content Project Editor: Natalie Griffith

Manufacturing Team Lead: Paul Herbert

National Geographic Liaison: Leila Hishmeh

Cover Designer: Natasa Arsenidou

Text Designer: eMC Design Ltd., UK and
    PreMediaGlobal

Compositor: PreMediaGlobal

Audio: EFS Television Production Ltd.

Acknowledgments
The publisher would like to thank the following
for their invaluable contribution: Nick Sheard,
Karen Spiller and Anna Cowper.

ISBN: 978-1-111-07117-2

National Geographic Learning
Cheriton House
North Way
Andover
Hampshire
SP10 5BW
United Kingdom

Cengage Learning is a leading provider of customised learning solutions with office locations around the globe, including Singapore, the United Kingdom, Australia, Mexico, Brazil and Japan. Locate our local office at:
international.cengage.com/region

Cengage Learning products are represented in Canada by Nelson Education, Ltd.

Visit National Geographic Learning online at **ngl.cengage.com**
Visit our corporate website at **cengage.com**

Photo credits

The publishers would like to thank the following sources for permission to reproduce their copyright protected photographs:

Cover photo: John Burcham/National Geographic Image Collection

pp 3a (Shutterstock.com), 3b (Roy McMahon/Corbis), 5 (Shutterstock.com), 6 (Shutterstock.com), 9a (Shutterstock.com), 9b (Shutterstock.com), 10a–b (Paul Corbit Brown. Courtesy of Need magazine), 11 (Jim Richardson/ National Geographic Image Collection), 14 (Shutterstock.com), 16 (Shutterstock.com), 18 (Hill Street Studios/Getty Images), 19 (Interfoto/Alamy), 20a (Yash Raj Films/The Kobal Collection), 20b (Central Press/Hulton Archive/Getty Images), 21 (Shutterstock.com), 32 (courtesy of Sylwia Gruchała), 33a (courtesy of Challenged Athletes Foundation), 33b (courtesy of Tim Mantoani Photography and Challenged Athletes Foundation), 35 (Shutterstock.com), 36 (Shutterstock.com), 40 (Robert Madden/National Geographic Image Collection), 41 (The Art Archive/Museum of London), 42a (klikk/ iStockphoto.com), 42b (Sportstock/iStockphoto.com), 43a (Shutterstock.com), 43b (Alaska Stock Images/National Geographic Image Collection), 44 (Shutterstock.com), 45 (Rich Reid/National Geographic Image Collection), 46a (Paul Sutherland/National Geographic Image Collection), 46b (Shutterstock.com), 53 (Shutterstock.com), 54a (Justin Guariglia/National Geographic Image Collection), 54b (Shutterstock.com), 56 (Shutterstock.com), 57 (Moodboard/123rf.com), 64 (mrloz/iStockphoto.com), 65a (Stephen Ferry/Getty Images), 65b (Moritz Steiger/The Image Bank/Getty Images), 65c (Reuters/David Gray), 66 (Photographers Direct/Richard Levine), 68 (Shutterstock.com), 76a (Jess Hurd/Reportdigital.co.uk), 76b (tseybold/iStockphoto.com), 77 (Olivier Asselin/Alamy), 80 (Shutterstock.com), 85 (Dod Miller/Alamy), 86a (Shutterstock.com), 86b (marcoregalia/iStockphoto.com), 87 (McArthur's Universal Corrective Map of the World. © 1979 McArthur. Available worldwide from ODT, Inc. (1–800–736–1293; www.ODTmaps.com; Fax: 413–549–3503; E-mail: odtstore@odt. org). Also available in Australia from McArthur Maps, 208 Queens Parade, North Fitzroy, 3068, Australia; Phone: 0011-613-9482–1055; Email: stuartmcarthur@hotmail.com), 88 (Shutterstock.com), 90 (Shutterstock.com), 96a (Lise Aserud/AFP/Getty Images), 96b (DAJ/Getty Images), 97a (Cathy Yeulet/123rf.com), 98a (Stephen Finn/123rf.com), 98b (Britain on View/Photolibrary.uk.com), 98c (Shutterstock.com), 99a (Fintastique/Dreamstime. com), 99b (Galantnie/Dreamstime.com), 100a (Kentoh/Dreamstime.com), 100b (Ingo Arndt/ Minden Pictures/National Geographic Image Collection), 100c (doug4537/iStockphoto.com), 100c (Lezh/iStockphoto.com), 101a (Shutterstock.com), 101b (Shutterstock.com), 102–103 (Kevin Schafer/National Geographic Image Collection), 104–105 (Kim Karpeles/Alamy), 104a (William Albert Allard/National Geographic Image Collection), 106–107 (Robert Clark / National Geographic Image Collection), 106a (Eye of Science / Photo Researchers, Inc.), 106b (GoodOlga/iStockphoto.com), 106c (by Robert H. Mohlenbrock), 106d (Shutterstock.com), 106e (Robert Clark/National Geographic Image Collection), 107a (Fuzzbass/Dreamstime.com), 107b (Robert Clark/National Geographic Image Collection), 108a (Shutterstock.com), 108b (Henrik5000/iStockphoto.com), 108c (Shutterstock.com), 109a (Shutterstock.com), 109b (Shutterstock.com), 110a (Bburgess/Dreamstime.com), 110b (Mary C Legg/alamy), 111a (Shutterstock.com), 111b (Gerd Ludwig/National Geographic Image Collection), 111c (Michael and Patricia Fogden/Minden Pictures/National Geographic Image Collection)

Illustrations by Sineval Almeida (pp 12, 22, 34, 58, 78), Peter Cornwell (pp 8, 55, 75, 85), Celia Hart (p 52), Martin Sanders (p 41), Mark Turner (pp 4, 30, 62)

Printed in the United Kingdom by Ashford Colour Press Ltd.
Print Number: 10   Print Year: 2024

The present

Grammar: present simple

1 **Complete the dialogue with the correct form of the verbs in brackets. Use short forms.**

Jack: Hello. I'm Jack.
¹ .... (you / go) to school here?

Holly: Yes, I ² .... (be) new here. I'm Holly.

Jack: ³ .... (you / like) it at Redhill High?

Holly: Yes. It's OK, but I ⁴ .... (not have) any friends here.

Jack: Yes, it can be difficult to make friends when you've just started a new school. I know, I've moved school three times! I ⁵ .... (have got) an idea. Do you like ⁶ .... (act)?

Holly: Yes, I do and I love ⁷ .... (sing), too.

Jack: How about ⁸ .... (join) the drama club?

Holly: Well, perhaps ...

Jack: I ⁹ .... (go) with my friends, Jenny and Paul. It's great fun.

Holly: How often ¹⁰ .... (you / go)?

Jack: We usually ¹¹ .... (practise) twice a week, on Monday and Thursday. The drama teacher sometimes ¹² .... (organise) extra rehearsals for the school play.

Holly: OK. Where ¹³ .... (the club / meet)?

Jack: In the school hall. Why don't you ¹⁴ .... (come) with me tomorrow afternoon?

Holly: Great. Thanks.

Jack: OK. See you here at half past three.

2 **Write questions in the present simple.**

1 How / you / get / school / ?
....

2 What time / Anna / have / breakfast / ?
....

3 How often / your friends / go / cinema / ?
....

4 When / Ryan / help / housework / ?
....

5 Diane and Kara / enjoy / study / maths / ?
....

6 Where / your / grandparents / live / ?
....

Grammar: present simple and present continuous

3 **Circle the correct option.**

1 It's raining / rains today.

2 Liane never wears / is never wearing make-up.

3 Farmers get up / are getting up early every morning.

4 Why don't you put up / putting up your umbrella?

5 Reporters often ask / are often asking a lot of questions.

6 A: Are you listening / Do you listen carefully to what I'm saying?
B: Yes, I do / am!

4 **Complete the text with the correct form of the verbs in the box.**

arrive	go (×2)	have got	learn	listen	not like
play	read (×2)	serve	watch	work (×2)	

Miranda is sixteen years old and goes to high school. She's a good student and ¹ .... hard, but she ² .... maths and science because she finds them a bit difficult. She loves ³ .... languages and ⁴ .... books. At the moment, she ⁵ .... a novel in French. After school, she ⁶ .... volleyball for the school or ⁷ .... to the leisure centre with her friends. On Saturdays, Miranda ⁸ .... a job in a supermarket in the town centre. She always ⁹ .... on time. She usually ¹⁰ .... in the fruit and vegetable section, but this month she ¹¹ .... customers in the bakery. On Saturday evenings, Miranda ¹² .... to the cinema or to a friend's house. They enjoy ¹³ .... DVDs or ¹⁴ .... to music together.

The past

Grammar: possessive forms

1 Complete the sentences with *have got*, a possessive adjective or apostrophe 's'.

1 It .... Alice .... birthday tomorrow.

2 John .... a new computer. It .... an AppleMac.

3 Sweden is a Scandinavian country. It .... capital is Stockholm.

4 My aunt .... two children. .... names are Miranda and Tom.

5 Tom .... the eldest. .... ambition is to be a doctor.

Grammar: articles

2 Complete the sentences with *the, a, an* or – (no article).

1 Do you like .... my new coat?

2 The receptionist is answering .... phone.

3 Tina usually eats .... orange in the afternoon.

4 What time do you usually go to .... bed?

5 Is there .... bank near here?

6 We can't swim in .... sea today! It's too cold.

Listening

3 *R.1* Listen to Claire and Ben talking about their birthdays. Choose the best picture (a or b).

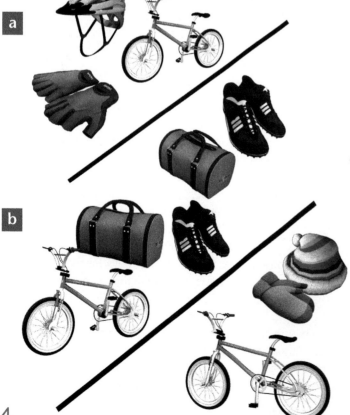

a

b

4 Complete the questions with the words in the box. Then listen to the dialogue again and answer the questions. Use each question word once.

How many	What	When	Where	Who	Why

1 .... did Claire get for her birthday?

....

2 .... bought it?

....

3 .... was Ben's birthday?

....

4 .... didn't he buy a new bike?

....

5 .... presents did Ben's parents give him?

....

6 .... did he go on his birthday?

....

5 Choose the correct option (a, b or c).

1 We saw a(n) .... film on Friday night.

   a amazing   **b** bored   **c** interested

2 I didn't enjoy the football match. It was ....

   a interesting   **b** tired   **c** boring

3 Marie Curie was .... in physics.

   a tired   **b** interested   **c** amazed

4 I went skiing ....

   a last two years **b** two years later **c** two years ago

5 They got married .... Saturday.

   a in   **b** last   **c** ago

6 My sister graduated from university .... she was twenty-two.

   a at   **b** while   **c** when

Giving opinions

6 Match the beginnings of the sentences (1–5) with the endings (a–e).

1 What did you   **a** with you.

2 I thought it   **b** sang really well.

3 No way! I think he   **c** opinion, Maria?

4 Me too. I agree   **d** think of his performance?

5 What's your   **e** was awful.

Describing and comparing

Reading

1 Read about Kate's first day at school. How did she feel?

a happy   **b** sad   **c** bored

I can remember when I started school. I was four years old. On the first day, my mum came with me. All the mums and children went into the classroom. The room was big and there were lots of pictures on the walls. There were lots of things to play with as well as paints and colouring pens. There was a wooden kitchen in one corner of the room and a huge sandbox in the other. I thought it was great. I also liked my teacher, Mrs Beniston. She was young and friendly. While my mum was talking to the teacher, I went over to the sandbox.
It was very noisy that morning. Most of the other children were crying and holding onto their mothers' legs. I couldn't understand why. After a while, the teacher asked all the mothers to leave. When my mum left the room, I didn't see her go because I was playing happily in the sand with another little girl. I think my mum was more upset than me about my first day at school.

2 Read the text again and answer the questions. Write full sentences.

1 Who went into the classroom with Kate?

....

2 What was the classroom like?

....

3 Where was the wooden kitchen?

....

3 Did Kate like her teacher?

....

5 What were many of the children doing?

....

6 What was Kate doing when her mum left the room?

....

7 Who was happier, Kate or the other children?

....

Grammar: comparatives

3 Complete the sentences with the correct form of the adjectives in the box.

bad	beautiful	heavy	hot	old	poisonous

1 I think snakes are .... than crocodiles. They've got such lovely skin!

2 A bus is .... than a motorbike.

3 Today, the weather is .... than yesterday. It's freezing and very windy.

4 The box jellyfish is one of the .... animals in the world.

5 It is too .... to go running this afternoon.

6 Max isn't .... enough to drive a car. He's still only sixteen.

4 Complete the questions with the correct comparative or superlative form of the adjective.

1 Australia / hot / New Zealand?

....

2 Which / big / country / in the world?

....

3 Who / good / actor / in your country?

....

4 a shark / dangerous / a whale?

....

5 Where / high / mountain / in the world?

....

6 Marie Curie / intelligent / her husband?

....

5 Circle the correct option (a, b or c).

Andorra is one of the [1] .... countries in Europe but it is probably one of [2] .... places for a holiday. In winter, you can go skiing in Andorra's [3] .... mountains. The ski resorts and villages are smaller [4] .... those in the Alps, but they are [5] .... and [6] .... relaxing. In the summer you can go rafting or canoeing. You can also go walking and trekking. Or you can sunbathe by the rivers and lakes. But don't jump in the water! It's always [7] .... cold to swim.

1	**a** smaller	**b** smallest	**c** small
2	**a** the best	**b** better	**c** good
3	**a** high	**b** tall	**c** large
4	**a** to	**b** as	**c** than
5	**a** friendly	**b** friendliest	**c** friendlier
6	**a** more	**b** enough	**c** too
7	**a** more	**b** too	**c** most

Shopping

Vocabulary

1 Circle the odd one out.

1 pasta   rice   cereals   fish

2 sweatshirt   jacket   helmet   jeans

3 yogurt   milk   onions   cheese

4 beans   chocolate   biscuits   crisps

5 shoes   gloves   sandals   boots

6 jar   tin   packet   sugar

Grammar: countable and uncountable

2 Circle the correct option for each sentence.

1 Are there *some / much / any* eggs in the fridge?

2 We have to buy *a / some / any* milk.

3 You can't make *any / an / some* omelette without eggs.

4 There wasn't *many / much / no* fresh fruit left in the shop.

5 How *much / many / lots of* sugar do you take in your coffee?

6 There were *much / no / any* customers in the shop.

Reading

3 Read the texts and choose the best heading (a–c) for each one. There is one extra heading.

a Shopping with my sister is fun

b Supermarket shopping is awful!

c I enjoy shopping with my mum

4 Complete the texts with the correct form of *have to* or *can*.

1 ....

I don't mind going to the supermarket with my mum. I ¹...................... go, but I know she likes me to help. We always go to the big supermarket outside the city centre. We take two shopping lists with us and divide the work. I ²...................... get all the things in jars and packets, like cereals, bread, rice or pasta. My mum ³...................... get the food from the cold section, like meat, fish, milk, cheese, etc. She also chooses the fruit and vegetables. There's a café in the supermarket and sometimes we have a cup of coffee and a cake before we go home.
Holly

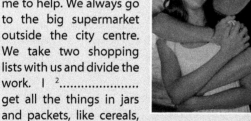

5 Read the texts again. Are the sentences true or false?

                                             T   F

1 When Holly goes to the supermarket she does nothing to help her mum. ☐ ☐

2 At the big supermarket there isn't anywhere for Holly and her mum to sit down. ☐ ☐

3 Holly's mum chooses the fresh food. ☐ ☐

4 James's mum buys enough food and drink for seven days. ☐ ☐

5 Everybody shops at the same supermarket in James's town. ☐ ☐

6 James puts everything away in the cupboards. ☐ ☐

7 Nobody helps James carry the shopping into the house. ☐ ☐

Grammar: *must, mustn't, can, can't* and *don't have to*

6 Read the signs and write the rules.

1 You / pay for / your shopping / here.

....

....

PAY HERE

2 Only / disabled people / park / here.

....

....

P ♿ **Disabled Parking**

3 You / buy / wine or beer / on Sundays.

....

....

No alcoholic drinks sold on Sundays

4 You / pay / in cash.

....

....

Cash only *No cards*

2 ....

I really hate shopping, but I ¹...................... go with my mum every Monday after school. I ²...................... walk home with my friends because she meets me after school in the car. We go to the small supermarket in the town centre. My little sister rides in the trolley and I ³...................... push it. My mum does all the shopping for one week, including heavy tins and bottles. All the people in our town shop there so it's always really busy. Then, we ⁴...................... wait in a very long queue to pay. When we get home I have to carry everything from the car and put it in the kitchen while mum puts it all in the cupboards. I do this on my own. My little sister ⁵...................... help, because she ⁶...................... lift the heavy bags.
James

Future forms

The future

1 Circle the correct option for each sentence.

Mum: I [1] *'m going to go / 'll go* to the shopping centre tomorrow.

Katy: Really? Can I come with you?

Mum: Of course you can.

Katy: What time [2] *will you leave / are you leaving*?

Mum: I [3] *'ll catch / 'm catching* the bus at 9 o' clock. If I don't go early, I [4] *don't have / won't have* time to do all my shopping.

Katy: That's too early for me! I think I [5] *'m staying / 'll stay* at home.

Mum: What [6] *will you do / are you doing* all day instead?

Katy: I'm not sure. Mike [7] *is playing / will play* in a hockey match. If it doesn't rain, I [8] *'m going to go / 'll go* and watch him.

Mum: OK. You [9] *'ll have to / having to* make your own lunch tomorrow. I [10] *'m going to get / get* something to eat in town.

Katy: Sure. Mum, can you buy some crisps and fizzy drinks? Holly [11] *will have / is having* a party tomorrow night.

Mum: I 'm sorry, Katy. I'm afraid I can't. I [12] *'m not going to do / won't do* any food shopping tomorrow. I'm going to buy a dress to wear at Anna's wedding.

2 Write sentences and questions with *will, going to* or present continuous. There is one example of each form.

1 A: Who / Tottenham play / on Sunday / ?

....

B: They / play / Manchester United.

....

2 A: Everybody / shop / online / in the future / ?

....

B: No, / people / still / go / shops and supermarkets.

....

3 A: When / you / do / your homework / ?

....

B: I / do / it / this evening.

....

Permission and advice

3 Read the dialogues and choose the correct option (a, b or c).

1 Rob: I'm sorry. I forgot to buy the drinks for the party.

Holly: Never mind. We can get some later.

What is Rob doing?
a asking for permission   **b** apologising
c giving advice

2 Kim: I went shopping yesterday, but I couldn't find any nice jeans.

Ben: You should go to Jeans Space in Market Street.

What is Ben doing?
a giving permission   **b** giving directions
c giving advice

3 Katy: Excuse me. Can I try these trainers on, please?

Assistant: Yes, of course. What size are you?

Katy: I'm a size 38.

What is the assistant doing?
a asking for information   **b** apologising
c giving advice

4 Jack: I'm afraid this jacket's too small. Have you got a bigger size?

Assistant: No, sorry. I'm afraid this is the biggest size we've got.

What is Jack doing?
a buying a jacket   **b** asking for a smaller jacket
c trying on a jacket

5 Tourist: Excuse me. Is the bus station near here?

Ben: Yes, it is. Go along Southgate and turn left at the end. It's on the right.

Tourist: Thank you.

What is Ben doing?
a giving directions   **b** catching a bus
c giving advice

4 Circle the correct option for each sentence.

1 How do I *arrive / go / get* to the museum?

2 Go *along / over / on* Park Road and turn right.

3 My legs *hurts / ache / pain* from walking round the shops all day.

4 You look tired. You *should / must / will* sit down for a while.

5 The art gallery is *down / opposite / next* the hotel.

6 What's *wrong / matter / happen* with you today?

1A A new life

Vocabulary: homes

1 Complete the puzzle and find the hidden word.

1 I share mine with my sister.

2 It's on the fifth floor.

3 We use the computers or my parents work in here.

4 This is where you take off your coat when you come through the front door.

5 It has lots of flowers and two small trees.

6 This house only has one floor.

7 Everyone sits in here to relax or watch TV.

8 We usually eat in here when we have guests.

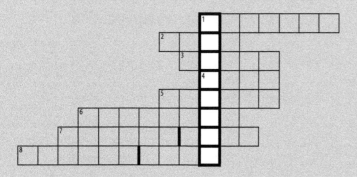

Hidden word: ....

2 Complete the descriptions of the rooms.

A This room is the ¹..................... The family spends a lot of time here and we eat most of our meals at the ²..................... It's always warm in here, but the dining room can be a bit cold! There's a ³..................... under the window and a ⁴..................... next to the cooker. We use this a lot to make warm drinks in the winter. It isn't a very big room, but there are lots of ⁵..................... on the wall to put food and dishes in. For me, the best thing in the room is the new ⁶..................... I hate doing the washing up!

B Our ¹..................... is really untidy. We keep all our ²..................... in here – we hang them on the ³...................... There are also lots of ⁴..................... on the wall with toys on them. On the ⁵..................... there are lots of boxes of books. My mum keeps asking my dad to move them into his study. We've got the ⁶.. in here, too because there isn't room for it in the kitchen. All this means that we can't put the ⁷..................... in here because there's no room! We park it in the street.

Grammar: present simple and verbs without a continuous form

3 Circle the verb that doesn't usually have a continuous form.

spend (hate) listen write

1 go out buy give understand

2 work eat live know

3 give buy need look

4 like win get leave

5 seem meet play come

6 learn prefer study choose

4 Complete the sentences with verbs from Exercise 3.

I *hate* food technology. It's too boring!

1 Maria and Andy .... very happy together. I think they're in love.

2 Do you .... the new French teacher? I think she's nice.

3 Mike is an excellent guide. He .... the city really well.

4 I live here. I don't .... a map!

5 Does Rosie .... coffee or tea?

6 Do you .... this maths question? It's really hard!

Vocabulary: personality adjectives

5 Complete the sentences with the adjectives in the box.

> funny   kind   lazy   patient   serious   strict

1 My parents are very .... They make me do extra homework every evening.

2 My brother is very hard-working, but I'm a bit ....

3 She always helps people and she's .... to animals.

4 Our maths teacher is .... He makes us laugh.

5 My sister never gets annoyed with her children. She's very ....

6 Our doctor is very .... He never smiles.

6 Write the opposite adjectives. Add *un-*, *im-* or *in-*.

friendly   *unfriendly*

1 competitive   ....
2 lucky   ....
3 polite   ....
4 mature   ....
5 fit   ....
6 comfortable   ....
7 correct   ....
8 important   ....

7 Complete the texts with the adjectives in the box. Use a negative prefix where necessary.

> competitive   fit   important   lazy   lucky   patient

A I'm Costa Rican, but my family live in New York now and I go to the New York School of Performing Arts (SPA). It's very difficult to get a place there, so I'm really [1] ....! At SPA, everyone studies music, acting and dance as well as the normal high school subjects. It's a very full timetable and can be tiring. Certainly, nobody at SPA is [2] .... – we spend all day moving about. We have to work hard at all school subjects though. The teachers get very [3] .... with students who don't work. Students who are really [4] .... have to leave the school. But this doesn't often happen because all the students are very [5] ...., including me. It's difficult to get a job in the performing arts, so it's [6] .... to work hard and be the best!

> correct   friendly   polite   strict   successful   tidy

B I'm from Tokyo in Japan. My family have a big apartment in a nice part of the city and I go to a private school. The rules at our school are very [1] .... We have to wear a school uniform and cut our hair in the same style. We always look smart and our hair is never [2] ....! I don't like the teachers though. They are serious and [3] .... Some of my teachers never smile!

In class, we have to get all the answers right to every exercise. If one answer is [4] ...., we have to do detention. We also get detention if we are [5] .... to the teacher. All of the students at my school study hard and get good marks in exams. Many students go to university and become [6] .... doctors or lawyers.

1 Look at the photos a and b. What are the children doing in each photo?

a

b

2 Read the article and check your answers to Exercise 1.

Students at the Nurani Insani Foundation in Jakarta, Indonesia love going to school. They are very enthusiastic and when the teacher asks a question, everybody's hand goes up. The students are also ambitious and want to become doctors and teachers. Nothing too unusual about that, you may think. But this is not an expensive, private school for rich kids. This is a school for street children.

The Nurani Insani Foundation was started by a university graduate called Achmad Dedi Rosadi because he wanted to help the street children. Every night, these children beg for money on the city's dangerous streets. Their parents do not work and depend on their children to earn money for the family. Rosadi knew that education was the only way to change the situation for the children's future, so he started teaching. He taught classes in the streets and under bridges but soon there were too many children. He needed a school, so he asked Indonesian people to donate money – which they did.

Rosadi now has his school and employs other teachers who share his ideas. The school timetable of lessons includes both academic and vocational subjects. As well as maths, English, Indonesian, geography, music and IT, the students also learn sewing, cooking and hairdressing. The school provides free school meals, and a doctor visits regularly. The uniform is free too, and the students look very smart in their white shirts. It makes them feel proud to be part of the school community. The school also wants the students to feel part of the wider community. They go on school trips to places like the airport and the zoo, in order to learn about the city they live in.

While the children are at school, they feel happy and safe. The school has given them hope and they are positive about the future. They want to find work in shops, offices or restaurants. Habil, 15, wants to be a police officer. His classmate, Desi, hopes to work as a secretary. But they also plan to continue studying after they leave school. 'I'm going to study online and get a degree,' says Desi. After school, they have to return to the streets, but at least they know it is not forever.

3 Read the text again and answer the questions.

1 Who goes to the Nurani Insani Foundation school?

2 Why do the students' parents depend on them?

3 Who started the school and why?

4 What three things does the school provide for free?

5 What are the students proud of?

6 What do Habil and Desi want to do when they leave school?

7 What do many of the students do after school?

Vocabulary: school subjects

4 Find nine school subjects in the text in Exercise 2 and complete the table.

Academic subjects	Vocational subjects
....	....
....	....
....	....
....	
....	
....	

5 Read the statements. Write the name of the school subject or the place.

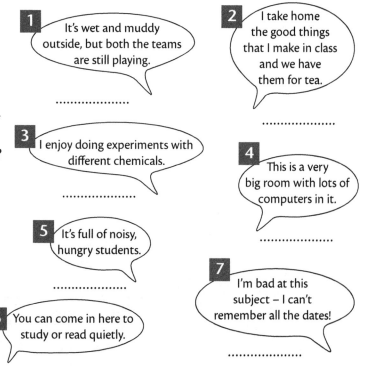

1 It's wet and muddy outside, but both the teams are still playing.

....

2 I take home the good things that I make in class and we have them for tea.

....

3 I enjoy doing experiments with different chemicals.

....

4 This is a very big room with lots of computers in it.

....

5 It's full of noisy, hungry students.

....

6 You can come in here to study or read quietly.

....

7 I'm bad at this subject – I can't remember all the dates!

....

Listening

6 🔘 *1.1* **Listen to Stacey. Where is she at the moment?**

a on a school trip in England

b on a trip to the mountains

c on a school trip in another country

7 **Listen again. Are the sentences true or false?**

	T	F
1 Stacey is on a geography trip.	☐	☐
2 In the mornings she goes to school.	☐	☐
3 The English students are helping to build a well for the local people.	☐	☐
4 The local students are good at music.	☐	☐
5 Her favourite school subjects are cooking and maths.	☐	☐
6 Stacey doesn't like the teachers at the school.	☐	☐
7 The teachers don't need to be strict.	☐	☐

Grammar: present simple and present continuous

8 **Read the uses of the present tenses (a–c). Match them with the correct examples (1–7).**

a An activity in progress at or around the time of speaking ....

b A regular or repeated activity *1*

c A state or feeling ....

1 My brother usually cooks dinner on Sunday.

2 Our hockey team are winning the league.

3 I don't really understand this exercise.

4 I love maths and chemistry.

5 The school year starts in September.

6 The students are designing a new webpage.

7 I need a new notebook.

9 **Complete the sentences with the correct form of the verbs in brackets.**

Stacey *is visiting* a school in Jakarta at the moment. (visit)

1 Our maths teacher .... us homework every day. (give)

2 Listen! The orchestra .... in the hall. (practise)

3 We can't do PE outside today because it .... (snow)

4 I .... good at maths. (not be)

5 The school bus .... at a quarter to nine every morning. (arrive)

6 Girls .... often more responsible than boys. (be)

Working with words: *do* or *make*

10 **Complete the sentences with the correct form of *do* or *make*.**

This restaurant *makes* the best pizzas in town!

1 Quiet, please! The students are .... an exam.

2 Jeremy is shy and doesn't .... friends easily.

3 The children always .... a mess when they play in the living room.

4 The school secretary .... a lot of phone calls every day.

5 My mum really hates .... the washing up. She wants to get a dishwasher!

6 I didn't .... any mistakes in the spelling test.

11 **Write questions using *do* or *make*.**

Can / you / a cake / ?

Can you make a cake?

1 How often / you / forget / your homework / ?

....

2 you / your bed / every morning / ?

....

3 What / mum / for lunch / today / ?

....

4 Where / Sally / gymnastics / ?

....

5 Who / drama / this term / ?

....

6 Can / you / the washing up / today, please / ?

....

Useful expressions

1 Complete the dialogues.

1 A: Hi, Keira. How are you?

B: I'm ...., thanks ....?

2 A: This is my friend, Cheryl.

B: .... meet you, Cheryl.

C: .... meet you, ...

3 A: Let me introduce my music teacher, Mr Singer.

B: How ....,
Mr Singer?

C: .... do,
Mrs Harris?

4 A: Hello Piers. This is your new headmaster, Mr Kane.

B: Pleased ...., Sir.

5 A: This is Sam's mum, Professor Smart.

B: .... do, Professor?

C: Please, ... Ruth.

2 Read each situation and choose the correct option (a, b or c).

1 Your dad is introducing you to his secretary, Mrs Johnson. What does your dad say?

a Hi, Mrs Johnson.

b Nice to meet you, Mrs Johnson.

c This is my secretary, Mrs Johnson.

2 You are greeting your maths teacher after the school holidays. What do you say?

a How do you do, Mr Woods?

b Hello, Mr Woods. How are you?

c Nice to meet you, Mr Woods.

3 Your sister is introducing her new friend, Darren. What do you say?

a Hi, Darren. Nice to meet you.

b This is Darren.

c I'm fine, thanks. And you?

3 Put the parts of the dialogue in the correct order.

☐ Amy: I'm great! I'm shopping for new shoes. Mum, this is Mel from the swimming club.

☐ Mel: OK. Pleased to meet you, Nicola.

[1] Amy: Hi, Mel. How are you?

☐ Mel: Nice to meet you too, Mrs Kidman.

☐ Amy's mum: Come on, Amy. The shops close in half an hour.

☐ Mel: I'm fine. And you?

☐ Amy's mum: Call me Nicola.

☐ Mel: OK. See you at training. Bye!

☐ Amy's mum: Hello, Mel. Nice to meet you.

☐ Amy: OK, Mum. Sorry, Mel. I've got to go. See you tomorrow.

SHOPPING

Pronunciation: weak forms /ə/

4 **1.2** Listen to the sentences. Is the underlined word stressed (S) or unstressed (U)?

1 I'm fine, thanks. <u>And</u> you?
2 Nice to <u>meet</u> you, Mrs Kidman.
3 How <u>do</u> you do, Mr Woods?
4 I'm shopping <u>for</u> new shoes.
5 See you at <u>training</u>.
6 The shops close in half <u>an</u> hour.

5 Listen again and practise saying the sentences.

Writing: a personal email

6 Read Yvonne's email. Complete the gaps (1–5) with *and* or *but*.

To: clare.sedgewick@mailit.uk
From: yvonne123@mailonline.uk
Subject: Our new home

Hello Clare,
How are you? How's everyone back in Billstown?
Our new house is fantastic. There are four bedrooms, so I've finally got my own room ¹ ....
I don't have to share it with Joanna! Mum spends a lot of time in her study because she's illustrating some children's books. She's really busy at the moment ² .... we see more of Dad. He doesn't need to catch the train to work anymore because he works in the same town.
My new school's OK. The people in my class are quite friendly ³ .... it's difficult to make friends because I'm shy. I'm lucky that Joanna is at the same school this year. She meets me at break ⁴ .... at lunchtime ⁵ .... I'm a bit worried. She's better at making new friends than me, so she'll soon have her own friends. I'm going climbing this weekend for the first time at a big climbing centre, so I can meet people from other schools.
I can hear dad coming in now, so I must go and help make the tea.
Love to everyone,
Yvonne

7 Match the beginnings of the sentences (1–6) with the endings (a–f).

1 Yvonne doesn't share a room with Joanna
2 Her mum needs to work a lot
3 Yvonne and her sister have lunch together
4 Joanna isn't shy
5 Yvonne is worried
6 Yvonne wants to meet people from other schools

a because her sister will soon have her own friends.
b so she makes friends more easily.
c because the new house is big.
d so she is joining a climbing club.
e so she spends a lot of time in her study.
f because they are at the same school.

8 Look at the questions and write notes.

1 Do you like your house or flat? Why / Why not?
2 Do you share a bedroom?
3 Who do you spend breaks and lunchtime with?
4 Have you got any new friends this term? Why / Why not?

9 Write an email to a penfriend. Include the information in Exercise 8. Remember to join your sentences with *and*, *because*, *but* and *so*.

Reading

1 Read and decide if sentences (a–d) are true (T) or false (F). Then complete sentences (e–f) with one word in each gap.

Kara lives on Saint Helena. It is a small island in the South Atlantic Ocean. She lives in a house in the capital, Jamestown, and goes to Prince Andrew School. It is the only high school on Saint Helena, so children go there from all over the island.
All the students wear a school uniform. Both the boys and the girls wear black trousers, a light blue shirt and a school tie. Sometimes the girls wear black skirts. All the students do maths, English, science and PE, but they can also choose four optional subjects. This year, Kara is studying art, geography, history, and design and technology. She likes all these subjects, but she enjoys science the most.

		T	F
a	There is only one high school on the island.	☐	☐
b	All the students have to study geography and history.	☐	☐
c	Kara doesn't like geography and history.	☐	☐

d Kara .... from Jamestown, on the island of Saint Helena.

e Kara's .... subject is science.

Listening

2 🔘 **1.3** You will hear four short statements twice. Match the statements with the correct response (a, b or c).

1 ....
a Nice to meet you.
b How are you?
c Fine thanks, and you?

2 ....
a Hello, Mum.
b Pleased to meet you, Mr Botts.
c Hi. I'm fine. And you?

3 ....
a Call me Angela.
b Fine thanks, and you?
c Hello. Nice to meet you.

4 ....
a Call me Joanna.
b See you later!
c No, thank you.

Word list Starter Unit and Unit 1

actually (adv) ....
aloud (adv) ....
annoyed (adj) ....
area (n) ....
as well as (phr) ....
assembly (n) ....
attend (v) ....
beg (v) ....
bungalow (n) ....
canteen (n) ....
cattle (n) ....
competitive (adj) ....
cover (v) ....
cry (v) ....
degree (n) ....
depend on (phr v) ....
detention (n) ....
disabled (adj) ....
donate (v) ....
employ (v) ....
enrol (v) ....
excellent (adj) ....
excursion (n) ....
folk (n) ....
folk (adj) ....
festival (n) ....
graduate (v) ....
guide (n) ....
hairdressing (n) ....
headmaster (n) ....
hockey (n) ....
important (adj) ....
in addition ....
introduce (v) ....
lawyer (n) ....

league (n) ....
lift (v) ....
lucky (adj) ....
mature (adj) ....
meal (n) ....
on one's own (phr) ....
opportunity (n) ....
ordinary (adj) ....
originally (adv) ....
outback (n) ....
patient (adj) ....
polite (adj) ....
proud (adj) ....
provide (v) ....
queue (n) ....
rapidly (adv) ....
rehearsal (n) ....
responsible (adj) ....
rowing (n) ....
rule (n) ....
sandbox (n) ....
seem (v) ....
serious (adj) ....
sewing (n) ....
share (v) ....
sheep *pl* sheep (n) ....
social networking site (n) ....
sports field (n) ....
stay in touch with (phr v) ....
strict (adj) ....
survive (v) ....
take part in (phr v) ....
tent (n) ....

though (adv) ....
three-storey house (n) ....
timetable (n) ....
tournament (n) ....
trolley (n) ....
urban area (n) ....
village (n) ....
vocational subject (n) ....
wooden (adj) ....

U1 Reading Explorer

announcement (n) ....
arts and humanities (phr) ....
bow (n) ....
cap (n) ....
ceremony (n) ....
cheer (v) ....
crown (v) ....
curtain (n) ....
date (n) ....
decorate (v) ....
details (n pl) ....
graduation (n) ....
horn (n) ....
line up (phr v) ....
march (v) ....
overalls (n) ....
patience (n) ....
ribbon (n) ....
speech (n) ....
tassel (n) ....
tradition (n) ....
tuxedos (n pl) ....

Grammar Practice | Unit 1

present simple

We use **present simple** to talk about:

- facts, general truths, laws of nature
  *Water **boils** at 100°C.*
- permanent states
  *My mum **works** in a bank.*
- regular habits
  *I usually **read** in the evening.*
- feelings and thoughts
  *I **love** reggae music.*

In the affirmative, we add **-s** to the verb after *he*, *she* or *it*. But with verbs ending in **-ss**, **-sh**, **-ch**, **-x** and **-o**, we add **-es**.
With verbs ending in a **consonant** + **-y**, we change the **-y** to **-ies**.

1 **Complete the short text with the present simple form of the verbs**

Australia *is* (be) a very big country, and the towns ¹ ...... (be) hundreds of kilometres apart. 12-year-old Janie Samson ² ...... (live) on a cattle station in the outback, far away from the nearest town, so she ³ ...... (not go) to school. She ⁴ ...... (have) lessons every day though – on the computer, using a satellite dish and a webcam. Every few months she ⁵ ...... (travel) to the city for special events with other outback students. She ⁶ ...... (enjoy) learning this way – but she ⁷ ...... (not like) doing homework!

2 **Complete the table with the verbs from Exercise 1.**

fact, general truth:	*is*	......
permanent state:	....	......
regular habit:	....	......
feeling, thought:	....	......

3 **Complete the sentences with the present simple form of the verbs.**

Karen *watches* (watch) TV every evening.

1 Zinah ...... (miss) some things about living in India.

2 My little brother often ...... (mix) up his words when he speaks.

3 Andy's always so tense – he ...... (worry) about everything!

4 Daisy sometimes (wish) ...... she was back in the USA.

5 Sharon ...... (go) shopping at least once a week.

6 My dad ...... (catch) the early train to London every day.

7 Matt ...... (do) a lot of extra activities at school.

8 Daisy's brother Luke never ...... (tidy) his room.

4 **Write negative sentences (✗) or questions (?).**

Jarek lives in Poland now. (✗)
Jarek doesn't live in Poland now.
Jack and Lauren often play tennis together. (?)
Do Jack and Lauren often play tennis together?

1 Lee wants to study medicine at university. (?)
....

2 Lee and Aneta live next door to each other. (✗)
....

3 Lauren plays the violin. (✗)
....

4 The four friends go to the same school. (?)
....

5 Aneta wants to be a dancer. (✗)
....

verbs without a continuous form

Some verbs are called 'stative' verbs because they describe a state, feeling or thought rather than an action. We DON'T normally use present continuous with these verbs. They include: *hate, know, like, love, need, prefer, seem, think, understand, want.*

present simple and present continuous

We use the **present simple** to talk about something that someone ***usually / often / always*** does, or about a permanent state.

We use the **present continuous** to talk about actions that are in progress now, at or around the time when we are talking, or about a temporary situation.

*Marco usually **lives** in Milan.*
*He's **living** in Florence at the moment.*

*My mum **works** in a bank.*
*She isn't **working** today – it's Saturday.*

5 **Complete the sentences with the correct form of the verbs.**

Matt *likes* (like) his new school.

1 Lauren's cousin ...... (stay) with her for a few days.

2 I ...... (not know) that word – I ...... (need) to use a dictionary.

3 Jack and Lauren ...... (play) tennis in the park at weekends.

4 Please don't make any noise – the baby ...... (sleep)!

5 Aneta usually ...... (go) to the theatre on Saturdays.

6 I ...... (think) Jack ...... (practise) the violin right now.

6 **Write sentences in the present simple or present continuous.**

I / know / Lee / really / like / Aneta

I know Lee really likes Aneta.

1 Jack / not play / with his group tonight, because / he / study

....

2 Matt / like / cooking and he / make / lots of different dishes

....

3 I / lie / on my bed at the moment and / listen / to music

....

4 Lauren / love / sports and she / play / in the hockey team

....

5 It / rain / very hard now, so we / wait / here for it to stop

....

6 Lee / usually / study / in the evenings but tonight he / take / a break

....

7 **Complete the questions with the present simple or present continuous form of the verbs in brackets.**

Does the team play (the team / play) a match every Saturday?

1 How often ...... (they / go) to the cinema?

2 ...... (Lauren / want) to join the rowing club?

3 ...... (you / believe) his story about what happened?

4 What ...... (you / listen) to? Is it your new CD?

5 What time ...... (the children / go) to bed?

6 Why ...... (Karen / cry)? Did someone upset her?

7 Who ...... (Dad / talk) to on the phone? He sounds angry!

8 ...... (you / remember) what homework we've got?

and, but, because, so

'Linking' words such as ***and, but, because*** and **so** are used to join two short sentences together into one longer sentence. The linking word shows a relationship between the main event/idea/etc in each of the two short sentences.

- ***and*** (two similar events/ideas)

  He likes reading. He is interested in sports.

  He likes reading and (he) is interested in sports.

- ***but*** (two opposite events/ideas)

  I can play the guitar. I can't play the piano.

  I can play the guitar but I can't play the piano.

- ***because*** (Sentence B gives the reason for Sentence A)

  The little boy felt sick. He ate a whole bar of chocolate.

  The little boy felt sick because he ate a whole bar of chocolate.

- ***so*** (Sentence B gives the result of Sentence A)

  The little boy ate a whole bar of chocolate. He felt sick.

8 **Match sentences 1-5 with sentences a–f.**

I'm studying maths tonight because I've got a test tomorrow.

I'm studying maths tonight. ⟍

1 Lauren plays tennis. ......

2 Aneta is Polish. ......

3 I'm really hungry. ......

4 Jack can play the piano. ......

5 Lee works hard at school. ......

a Mum's making me a pizza.

b He can't sing very well.

c I've got a test tomorrow.

d Now she lives in England.

e She's in the hockey team.

f He wants to become a doctor.

2A Hip-hop planet

Vocabulary: music

1 Complete the definitions with the style of music.

Gospel is a powerful style of American music that started in the African American coummunity.

1 Duke Ellington, Myles Davis and Chet Baker are all famous j................... musicians.

2 P.................... and d.................... music are often played at parties and discos.

3 There are many famous r................... bands, but my favourite is still The Rolling Stones.

4 Chopin and Mendelssohn were composers of c.................... music.

5 Mozart wrote o.................... music, including *The Marriage of Figaro* and *The Magic Flute*.

6 J.................... is a type of electronic music. The drum and bass line is very important.

2 Circle the correct option.

I can't stand Mika's music. I think it's (awful) great.

1 It's easy to sing Abba songs. They're really *catchy / exciting*.

2 I'm not sure if I like Bjork's music. It's very *strange / relaxing* and different.

3 The theme music to the film *Titanic* was *aggressive / romantic*.

4 That music is too *sad / loud*. Can you turn it down, please?

5 Blues songs are sometimes too *sad / happy*.

6 Soul music is brilliant. It's never *catchy / boring*.

Working with words: nouns → adjectives

3 Make adjectives from the nouns in the box and write them in the correct place in the table.

| artist | classic | danger | environment | interest |
| poison | ~~power~~ | success | symbol | talent |

-ful	-ed	-ous	-ic	-al
powerful				

4 Write the adjectives from the nouns.

1 adventure ....   4 fame ....

2 beauty ....   5 music ....

3 energy ....   6 virus ....

5 Complete the sentences with a noun or an adjective from Exercises 3 and 4.

1 The concert was .... Everybody really enjoyed it.

2 My grandad is very .... for his age. He goes running and works in the garden.

3 .... infections, like colds and flu, are common in winter.

4 He was born with a great .... for painting and drawing.

5 Ewan is very .... He enjoys doing extreme sports and travelling to wild places.

6 His sports car has a very .... engine – it can go as fast as 250 km per hour!

Grammar: *there was / there were*

6 Rewrite the second sentence so that it means the same as the first sentence. Use the correct form of *there was* or *there were*.

The theatre was empty.
There wasn't anybody in the theatre.

1 The DJ had two turntables.
.... two turntables for the DJ.

2 They didn't play any dance music at the party.
.... no dance music at the party.

3 They gave us a lot of food at the party.
.... a lot to eat at the party.

4 The concert didn't attract a big audience.
.... many people in the audience.

5 Did the group have a good drummer?
.... a good drummer in the group?

6 He didn't record any bad songs on his new album.
.... no bad songs on their new album.

Grammar: past simple and past continuous

7 Complete the sentences with the correct tense of the verbs in brackets.

Mozart *composed* his first piece of music when he was five years old. (compose)

1 When she looked out of the window, she saw it .... hard. (snow)

2 When I arrived at the party last night, everybody .... to hip-hop music. (dance)

3 We .... Joel a CD for his birthday. (buy)

4 He .... to the teacher, he was looking out of the window! (not listen)

5 .... the talent competition on TV last Saturday? (you / watch)

6 I .... my tea, then I .... to choir practice. (have / go)

8 Match the beginnings of the sentences (1–6) with the endings (a–f).

1 I fell asleep ...*d*...

2 American jazz was popular in England ......

3 While we were watching the concert, ...

4 When I was on holiday in Ireland, ...

5 The robbers stole the computers ......

6 Beethoven was writing an opera ......

a I learned some traditional dances.

b during the Second World War.

c when he died.

d during the film.

e two fans jumped onto the stage.

f during the night.

9 Complete the sentences with *when, while* or *during*, or the past simple or continuous form of the verbs in brackets.

Bob Marley grew up in Jamaica.[1] .... the 1960s. He [2] .... (leave) school at fourteen and worked in a factory, but he [3] .... (spend) all his free time playing reggae music with his friends. They formed a band called The Wailers and [4] .... (record) many successful singles in Jamaica. Bob and his friends were Rastafarians and [5] .... (believe) strongly in peace, love and human rights. During this time, Bob Marley [6] .... (begin) wearing his hair in long dreadlocks as a symbol of his Rastafarian beliefs.

In 1974, The Wailers [7] .... (break up). The other musicians [8] .... (leave) the band, but Bob Marley continued performing. He called his new band Bob Marley and the Wailers. In 1975 [9] .... the band had their first international hit with a song called *No Woman, No Cry*, Bob Marley decided to move to England.
[10] .... he was in England, he [11] .... (make) two more albums – *Exodus* and *Kaya*. These albums sold millions of copies and made reggae music popular worldwide.

In 1977, Bob Marley's doctors told him he had cancer, but because of his Rastafarian beliefs, he didn't want to take any medicine. He continued performing in concerts and recording his music. One day in 1980, [12] .... he [13] .... (fly) home to Jamaica, he [14] .... (become) very ill. The plane [15] .... (land) in Miami and he went to hospital. Bob Marley [16] .... (die) a few days later, aged thirty-six. He was buried in Jamaica with the things that were most important to him – his guitar and a Bible.

Reading

1 Read the article and choose the best photo (a or b) for the text.

a

b

Welcome to Bollywood

It is a hot June night in Mumbai, India. A group of people in colourful costumes is dancing round a big bonfire in front of a temple. There are fairy lights and other decorations everywhere. Two young actors are performing in front of an enormous film crew. They are lip-synching to a catchy song. The place is Film City outside Mumbai, a huge area of studios and film sets with everything from fantastic palaces and temples to city slums and poor villages. The two actors are the stars of *Veer-Zaara*, the latest film by one of Bollywood's most famous film directors, Yash Chopra. For *Veer-Zaara*, Chopra has recreated his home state of Punjab, in the north of India, in Film City and has brought dancers from Punjabi villages to perform in the film. The story of the film is a typical, romantic Bollywood tale: boy meets girl and they fall in love but, of course, their families are not happy about it and don't want them to marry.

Bollywood is India's answer to Hollywood. The only difference is that all the films are musicals. During the 1960s and '70s, Yash Chopra introduced many of the features that are now traditional in Bollywood films: romantic plots, fantastic costumes, catchy songs and amazing sets. However, the true stars of Bollywood are the songs and the music. The songs are known as 'filmi' and the singers are some of India's most talented performers.

Everyone in India, from the very young to the very old, loves filmi. You can hear filmi hits and golden classics on radios everywhere, from taxis to street stalls. The singers and musicians record and release the music before the film opens in cinemas and the songs become hits before the films even reach the screens. Some people go to see a film over and over again, just so that they can listen to their favourite songs. Whilst richer families can stay at home and watch the films on DVD, in poorer villages, the cinemas are full night after night. The cinema building is often just a large tent and a projector but the tickets cost about 25 cents – a small price to pay for a few hours of Bollywood magic.

2 Read the article again. Are the sentences true or false?

		T	F
1	The young actors are decorating the temple.	☐	☐
2	The buildings in Film City are not real.	☐	☐
3	Bollywood films are musicals and usually have a romantic plot.	☐	☐

		T	F
4	It is the actors in the films who sing the hit film songs (filmi).	☐	☐
5	Radio stations play songs from new films before they reach the cinemas.	☐	☐
6	In rich villages, people meet in a tent to watch DVDs.	☐	☐

Listening

3 ⊙ **2.1** Listen to Pradip talking about Indian pop music. Tick (✓) the words you hear.

American pop artists ☐   Bhangra ☐
Bollywood ☐   hip-hop ☐   filmi ☐
local music shops ☐

4 Listen again and complete the notes.

Interview notes
— Pradip enjoys listening to dance music and Indian pop music.
— There are two types of modern music mixed with traditional Indian music: Indi-pop and Bhangra.
— ¹ .... combines traditional music from the ² .... region of India and electronic dance music. Indian music has influenced a lot of ³ .... singers, such as Missy Elliot and Britney Spears.
— Pradip also likes music by the rock group ⁴ ....
— They mix traditional Indian instruments like sitars and Indian ⁵ .... with soul, funk and rock music.
— 'Indie band' means that Cornershop are independent and you can only buy their albums in local music shops or on the ⁶ ....

Working with words: verbs →nouns

5 Circle the correct option.

1 The theatre group put on a great *performer / performance* last night.
2 Did you see the Picasso *exhibition / exhibit*?
3 Can you help me with my *scientist / science* homework, please?
4 The Italian *competitors / competition* were late, so they didn't take part in the race.
5 Acting is about the *communication / communicate* of emotion to an audience.

6 Complete the sentences with the correct form of the words in the box.

| appear compete construct ~~paint~~ perform pollute sing |

My favourite *painting* is *Sunflowers* by van Gogh.

1 In big cities, there is a lot of .... from cars and factories.
2 My cousins are in a choir, but their .... is awful!
3 Leona Lewis won Britain's biggest talent .... in 2008.
4 Hitchcock made a(n) .... in his films.
5 Even very experienced .... are often nervous before they go on stage.
6 The .... of the film set took six months.

Grammar: present perfect

7 Complete the table with the irregular verb forms.

infinitive	past simple	past participle
be	....	....
....	....	got
have	....	....
....	knew	....
make	....	....
....	....	sold
....	sang	....
take	....	....
win	....	....
write	....	....

8 Complete the text with the correct present simple or present perfect form of the verbs in brackets.

Avril Lavigne is a Canadian singer, songwriter and actress. She *has made* (make) three top-selling albums and ¹ .... (sell) more than 30 million albums. Avril always ² .... (write) all her own songs on her albums and ³ .... usually .... (not record) songs by other songwriters. Her style of music is a mixture of pop, rock and punk rock. She ⁴ .... (win) lots of awards and ⁵ .... (have) five number-one singles, including *Sk8er Boi* and *Girlfriend*. Avril regularly ⁶ .... (perform) in concerts all over the world and ⁷ .... (sing) on stage several times with Shania Twain. She ⁸ .... also .... (appear) in several films, including *Sabrina the Teenage Witch* and *The Flock*, with Richard Gere. Her other interests include fashion and working for charities. Today she ⁹ .... (design) clothes for her clothing company, Abbey Dawn. Like a lot of famous people these days, she ¹⁰ .... also .... (release) her own perfume, called 'Black Star'.

Useful expressions

1 **Match the beginnings of the expressions (1–9) with the endings (a–i).**

1 I'm phoning about   **a** does the concert start?

2 I'm afraid   **b** for your help.

3 How much   **c** tickets for the concert on Saturday.

4 What time   **d** I help you?

5 Thanks   **e** a moment, please?

6 Can you hold on   **f** phone back later?

7 How can   **g** we've only got tickets for Friday.

8 You're   **h** do the tickets cost?

9 Can I   **i** welcome.

2 **Complete the dialogue with some of the expressions in Exercise 1.**

Natalie: Look at this poster! There's a Cornershop concert on this week.

Lisa: Great! I love their music. Let's get tickets for Saturday.

Natalie: OK. I'll phone the number now. Let's see 01382 7448576. It's ringing.

Salesman: Hello. Ticket office. ¹ ....
....?

Natalie: Hello. I'm phoning about tickets for the Cornershop concert on Saturday.

Salesman: ² ....

Natalie: Oh. Friday's a school day and we don't live in the city. ³ ....?

Salesman: At seven o'clock, but you need to be here early to get a good seat.

Natalie: Yes, of course. I need to talk to my friend. ⁴ ....?

Salesman: Of course.

Natalie: ⁵ ....

Salesman: You're welcome.

3 🔊 *2.2* **Listen to four statements and choose the correct response.**

1 ....

  a Sorry. There aren't any tickets left.

  b How much do the tickets cost?

  c I'm phoning about tickets for tonight's show.

2 ....

  a They're £45 each.

  b It starts at eight o'clock.

  c Sorry, there aren't any tickets left.

3 ....

  a You're welcome.

  b The tickets are too expensive.

  c Yes, of course.

4 ....

  a Yes, of course.

  b You're welcome.

  c Goodbye.

GREAT CONCERT WITH CORNERSHOP 25th October

Pronunciation: the sounds /t/ and /d/ before /j/

4 Say the statements. Underline the words joined by the sound /ts/ or /dz/.

1 Have you <u>bought your</u> ticket?
2 Did you enjoy the film last night?
3 Did you buy an Avril Lavigne album last year?
4 This is Anna. She arrived yesterday from England.
5 My costume is ready, but yours isn't.
6 Let's invite your brother to the party.

5 **2.3** Listen and check. Then practise saying the statements.

Writing: a diary

6 Complete Natalie's diary entry. Circle the correct linking words.

Saturday	October **25**

I had a great time last night! I went to see Cornershop in concert. They were brilliant! I went with Lisa and her sister, Leila. ¹ *After that / After* school, Leila picked us up in her car and we drove into the city centre. We arrived about five o'clock. ² *First / Before*, we had something to eat in a café. ³ *After / Then*, we walked to the concert hall. We joined the big queue outside and waited for ages to get in. We were worried about finding good seats because there were so many people in front of us. ⁴ *In the end / Before*, we stood at the front, near the stage. ⁵ *While / During* the concert, everyone was dancing and singing. It was brilliant! The concert finished at about 10 o'clock. ⁶ *Before / Then* we left the concert hall, we had a drink in the bar. ⁷ *During / After that*, Leila drove us back home and Lisa and I fell asleep in the car.

CORNERSHOP
in concert
25 October, City Concert Hall,
Ticket price: £25

7 You have been on a trip to Paris with your friends. Use the prompts below to write about it. Expand the ideas into full sentences and use the linking words in the boxes in the gaps.

after that	first	then

Saturday, / I got up six o'clock. / …. / had shower / …. / I had some breakfast. / …. / my dad / took me / station / where / met my friends

On Saturday, I got up at six o'clock. First, I had a shower. ....
....
....

after	then	when

We caught / London–Paris train / half past seven. / …. / we arrived in Paris. / we took metro to Musée d'Orsay. / We bought tickets and / …. / we had a second breakfast / museum café. / …. / breakfast / we went into museum / look at paintings.

....
....
....
....
....

after that	in the end	while

/ …. / I / was looking at / Impressionist paintings, / the others moved / another gallery. / I looked everywhere for them, / but I couldn't find them! / …. / I / found them / in café at the top of building. / …. / we all went look at modern art exhibitions.

....
....
....
....
....

8 Think of a day when you went to see a show, a concert or an exhibition. Write notes to answer these questions.

1 Where did you go?
2 When did you go?
3 Who did you go with?
4 How did you get there?
5 What did you do when you arrived?
6 What did you do next?
7 Where did you sit? / What did you see?
8 What did you do at the end of the day?

9 In your notebook, write a diary entry for your day. Use your notes from Exercise 8 and add linking words.

Reading

1 Read the text and choose the correct option.

> James Brown is famous as 'The Godfather of Soul'. He was one of the most famous soul singers in the world. He had a powerful voice and was an energetic performer. During his career he introduced new styles and inspired many other singers, including Michael Jackson. James Brown's soul music has been a big influence on famous rappers, such as Chuck D and LL Cool J.

What is the text about?

a James Brown's influence on modern music
b James Brown's biggest hits
c James Brown's rap music

2 Read the text and choose the correct option.

> Wales has a strong musical tradition and it is often called 'The Land of Song'. It has a history of brass bands, folk music and, more importantly, choirs. Every year, Wales holds the largest festival of music and poetry competitions in Europe. The National Eisteddfod of Wales takes places over eight days and all the performances are in Welsh. The festival has always been very popular. Each year, there are around 6,000 competitors and about 150,000 visitors.

What is the text about?

a the history of Wales
b music in Wales
c Welsh folk festivals

Listening

2 ⊙ 2.4 Listen to the recorded message and complete the missing information.

TICKET OFFICE

Opening hours: ¹ .... a.m. to 6 p.m.
Monday to ² ....

Tickets for ³ .... performances of *Fame* are sold out.
Tickets cost ⁴ £ .... and £45
20% discount for ⁵ ....

3 ⊙ 2.5 Listen to the information about a singer and complete the information.

1 She was born in ....
2 She started writing songs when she was ....
3 Her first single sold .... copies.
4 She recorded her first album in ....

4 ⊙ 2.6 Listen and complete the form.

Schools' Eisteddfod Festival
Competition Entry Form

Name of act: ¹ *Bangor* .... *choir*
Number of performers: ² ....
Category: ³ .... *music*
Entry fee: ⁴ ....

Word list Unit 2

across (prep)	....	exhibition (n)	....	rehearse (v)	....
amazing (adj)	....	experience (n)	....	release (v)	....
appear (v)	....	extreme (adj)	....	repetitive (adj)	....
argument (n)	....	facility (n)	....	run away (phr v)	....
audience (n)	....	factory (n)	....	sculptor (n)	....
authorities (n pl)	....	fall in love (phr v)	....	sculpture (n)	....
belief (n)	....	fashionable (adj)	....	skull (n)	....
believe (v)	....	feature (n)	....	slum (n)	....
bonfire (n)	....	fight (n)	....	social life (n phr)	....
break up (phr v)	....	get on with (phr v)	....	spot (n)	....
bully (n)	....	grow up (phr v)	....	stall (n)	....
bury (v)	....	hill (n)	....	taste (v)	....
carry on (phr v)	....	hold on (phr v)	....	temple (n)	....
case (n)	....	however (conj)	....	trumpeter (n)	....
cellist (n)	....	human (adj)	....	turntable (n)	....
century (n)	....	include (v)	....	viral (adj)	....
childhood (n)	....	injury (n)	....	world-famous (adj)	....
choir (n)	....	interview (n)	....	worldwide (adj)	....
common (adj)	....	invite (v)	....	**U2 Reading Explorer**	
conductor (n)	....	involve (v)	....	alternative (n)	....
crew (n)	....	jewellery (n)	....	attract (v)	....
crime (n)	....	join (v)	....	brilliant (adj)	....
cut off (phr v)	....	keep (v)	....	fringe (n)	....
design (v)	....	lip-synch (v)	....	prestigious (adj)	....
develop (v)	....	own (pron)	....	shocking (adj)	....
director (n)	....	performer (n)	....	spectacular (adj)	....
discover (v)	....	period (n)	....	take part (phr v)	....
during (conj)	....	plot (n)	....	take place (phr v)	....
empty (adj)	....	poor (adj)	....	unofficially (adv)	....
enter (v)	....	prodigy (n)	....		
evidence (n)	....	recent (adj)	....		

Grammar Practice Unit 2

there was / there were

We use *there was* (with **singular** or **uncountable** nouns) and *there were* (with **plural** nouns) to describe what was in a place at a particular time in the past.

The negative form is *there wasn't* and *there weren't*.

We make questions with *Was there* and *Were there*.

There was a concert yesterday. (singular)

There wasn't any food. (uncountable)

Were there any good shops? (plural)

1 **Choose the correct words.**

There *was* / ~~were~~ a great new music programme on TV last night.

1 There *was / were* some good songs on the CD.

2 We couldn't go to the concert. There were *any / no* tickets left.

3 There *were / weren't* any cars in the 1500s.

4 *Was / Were* there any rap music at the party?

5 There weren't *any / some* MP3 players when he was a child.

6 There was *an / some* information about the group on the Internet.

past simple and past continuous

We use **past simple** to talk about:

• actions, events or states which started and finished in the past.

• habits in the past, which are now finished.

• a number of actions in the past which happened one after the other.

We use **past continuous** to talk about actions that were in progress at a specific time.

2 **Choose the correct words.**

He *learned* / ~~was learning~~ the violin when he was a young child.

1 Tina *was still listening / still listened* to music at midnight.

2 She *picked / was picking* up the microphone and began singing.

3 Jazz *was starting / started* in America about 100 years ago.

4 What *did you do / were you doing* at this time yesterday?

5 Until I was about 15 I *hated / was hating* classical music.

when, while and during

We can use *when* + **past simple** or *while* + **past continuous** to talk about the two actions together.

I was listening to music when my friend called.

My friend called while I was listening to music.

We use **past simple** with *during* + **noun phrase** to talk about actions that started and finished within a longer period of time in the past.

During the 20th century, technology advanced a lot.

3 **Complete the sentences with *when, while* or *during*.**

When the first lesson started she was still having breakfast.

1 I was having a shower ...... the phone rang.

2 Unfortunately there was a huge storm ...... the open-air concert.

3 He started recording songs ...... he was working as a waiter.

4 Everyone started cheering ...... the group walked onto the stage.

5 I heard this same song on the radio ...... I was having breakfast.

4 **Complete the sentences with the past simple or past continuous form of the verbs.**

He *stood* (**stand**) up and *left* (**leave**) the room.

1 Rap music ...... (**begin**) during the late 1970s.

2 The show ...... (**start**) while we ...... (**still / wait**) to get in.

3 I ...... (**watch**) TV when they ...... (**announce**) the news about Michael Jackson's death.

4 The teacher ...... (**not leave**) the classroom while the students ...... (**do**) the test.

5 Aneta ...... (**sleep**) when Lee ...... (**arrive**)

present perfect

We use the **present perfect** to talk about:

• actions that happened in the past, but exactly when the action happened is not known or not important.

• states that began in the past and continue up to the present.

We form the present perfect with *have* or *has* and the **past participle** of the main verb.

Irregular verbs do not form the past participle by adding *-ed*. They have a different past participle form

We can use the word *ever* in present perfect questions; it goes before the main verb.

*Have you **ever** been to Manchester?*

We can form negative sentences in the present perfect with the word ***never***; it goes before the main verb.

*Sophie has **never** listened to rap music.*

5 **Complete the sentences with the present perfect form of the verbs.**

Mum *has made* (**make**) a chocolate cake.

1 I ...... (speak) to Lee's brother on the phone a few times, but I ...... (never meet) him.

2 Jack ...... (appear) in several concerts with his folk group.

3 I ...... (watch) her videos on TV, but I ...... (not see) her perform live.

4 Aneta ...... (write) a lot of short stories, and she ...... (be) in the school play a couple of times.

5 Lauren ...... (play) tennis with Jack for years, but she ...... (never beat) him.

6 **Write sentences or questions in the present perfect using these words.**

Jack / ever / live / in another country / ?

Has Jack ever lived in another country?

1 Vanessa-Mae / ever / perform / in your country / ?

....

2 I / never / buy / any of her music

....

3 Lauren / never / want / to learn the piano

....

4 you / ever / try / skateboarding / ?

....

5 many people / never / be / to a classical music concert

....

first, then, after, after that, before, during, in the end

'Linking' words/phrases are used to show the sequence of two or more actions/events.

- ***first, then*** and ***after that*** are used with two or more actions/events happening one after the other. We begin the sentence with the linking word/phrase, followed by **subject + verb**.

  ***First** I finished my homework. **Then** I had dinner. **After that**, I watched TV.*

- ***before, during*** and ***after*** compare the sequence of two actions or events.

  ***Before** I had dinner, I finished my homework. **During** dinner, we decided what film to see. **After** dinner, we went to the cinema.*

- ***in the end*** introduces an action/event which followed some action(s)/event(s) already mentioned.

  *I started watching a comedy series, but I got bored. **In the end**, I watched an old Western.*

7 **Choose the correct words.**

Yesterday wasn't a great day at school. First we had French. [1] *Then / After* it was history, and it was really boring. [2] *After / After that* we had maths, which I hate. [3] *Then / After* maths it was science, which is usually OK – but yesterday we had a test. [4] *Before / During* the test started, I couldn't remember anything. [5] *Then / During* the test I started to relax, though, and I answered almost all of the questions. [6] *After that / In the end* I got the best mark in the class!

Review Units 1 and 2

Grammar: comparing

1 **Complete the second sentence so that it means the same as the first sentence. Use the correct form of the words in brackets.**

1 Our school is less traditional than your school.
Our school is .... (modern)

2 Chemistry is less interesting than physics.
Physics isn't .... (as / boring)

3 Diane isn't as good at maths as Rosie.
Rosie is .... (good)

4 My mother's cooking is worse than the food at school!
The food at school isn't ....
.... (as / bad)

5 The teachers here are not as strict as the teachers at my old school.
The teachers at my old school were ....
.... (strict)

6 A Banksy painting is not as expensive as a Damien Hirst painting.
A Banksy painting is ....
(less / expensive)

7 My school uniform is the same as your school uniform.
Your school uniform isn't ....
.... (different)

8 The students in this class are not as quiet as the students in the maths class.
These students .... (noisy)

2 marks per item: ...... / 16 marks

2 **Write the second sentence so that it means the same as the first. Use *not as much / many as* OR *more than*.**

students / on sports field / than / in the classroom.
There are more students on the sports field than there are in the classroom.

1 facilities / in large schools / than / in small schools.
There ....

2 not as / posters / in my bedroom / as / in your bedroom.
There ....

3 tracks / on Coldplay's new album / than / their old album.
There ....

4 not as / furniture / in our house / as / in your house.
There ....

5 milk / in your glass / than / in my glass.
There ....

2 marks per item: ...... / 10 marks

Present simple or present continuous

3 **Complete the sentences with the correct form of the verbs in the box.**

| listen know need prefer understand work |

1 I .... how to dance the salsa.

2 There are holes in my shoes. I ....
some new shoes.

3 Be quiet! Harriet .... on the computer.

4 Tina and Susie .... to music in their bedroom at the moment.

5 .... you .... jazz or soul music?

6 I don't .... the instructions to this exercise.

1 mark per item: ...... / 6 marks

Past simple or past continuous

4 **Complete the sentences and questions with the correct form of the verbs in brackets.**

1 There .... (be) thousands of dancers at the Bollywood film studio yesterday.

2 .... (be) there a maths test last week?

3 Who .... (win) the singing competition last Saturday?

4 We .... (play) hockey on the sports field when it .... (start) to rain.

5 The violinist's string .... (broke) while she .... (play) on stage.

6 What .... (you / do) after school yesterday?

1 mark per item (verb): ...... / 8 marks

5 **Complete the text with the correct form of the verbs in brackets.**

My great-grandfather [1] .... (leave) school when he [2] .... (be) eleven years old and [3] .... (get) a job. He loved music and in the evenings he [4] ....
(teach) himself to play the trumpet and to speak German. He [5] .... (meet) my grandmother during the war when he [6] .... (work) as a secret agent in France. When the war [7] .... (finish), he [8] .... (return) to England and [9] .... (become) a jazz musician. Last year, my sister [10] .... (finish) writing a book about his amazing life.

1 mark per item: ...... / 10 marks

Vocabulary: home and school

6 **Complete the lists with words in the box.**

armchair	fridge	toilet	wardrobe	whiteboard

1 Classroom: desks, chairs, ...
2 Kitchen: cooker, dishwasher, ...
3 Bedroom: bed, lamp, ...
4 Bathroom: bath, mirror, ...
5 Living room: sofa, TV, ...

1 mark per item: ...... / 5 marks

7 **Write the school subjects.**

1 You study drawing and painting. ....
2 Biology, chemistry and physics are all examples of this. ....
3 You learn how to use computers. ....
4 You learn about the past. ....
5 You make different dishes. ....

1 mark per item: ...... / 5 marks

Music and performing

8 **Circle the odd one out.**

1 cellist   guitarist   trumpeter   violinist
2 turntable   harp   DJ   rapper
3 awful   catchy   great   exciting
4 drummer   guitarist   singer   conductor
5 choir   soloist   orchestra   band

1 mark per item: ...... / 5 marks

Nouns and adjectives

9 **Complete the sentences with nouns or adjectives.**

1 She never smiles or says hello. She's very u...................... .
2 William is really c..................... . He always wants to win.
3 Did you see Penny's p..................... last night? She sang beautifully.
4 Sean never does any work. He's so l..................... .
5 The chairs in our classroom are hard and u..................... .
6 The students are having an art e..................... at the school this week.
7 I live in a big industrial city where there's a lot of air p..................... .
8 I got an 'A' in my maths exam. Only one calculation was i..................... .

9 My parents pay for me to have extra lessons. They think e.................... is very important.
10 Sally plays the violin extremely well. She's a very t.................... musician.

1 mark per item ...... / 10 marks

Do or make

10 **Complete the sentences with the correct form of *do* or *make*.**

1 Oh no! The children .... a terrible mess! Tell them to stop it now!
2 How many mistakes .... in the test yesterday?
3 Last term, we .... a project on Asian music.
4 My mum usually cooks the supper and my dad .... the washing up.
5 Don't .... a noise. The baby is sleeping.

2 marks per item: ...... / 10 marks

Linking words

11 **Circle the correct option to complete the story.**

Last week, I went to the cinema with my friends to see *High School Musical III*. We waited outside for nearly an hour [1] *so / because* the queue was very long. [2] *When / Then* we got to the ticket office, there weren't any tickets left. [3] *First / Next*, we thought about seeing a different film [4] *but / and* we didn't like any of them. [5] *After / In the end*, we decided to go to the later showing, at 7.30 p.m.

1 mark per item: ...... / 5 marks

Asking for information

12 **Gavin is phoning the ticket office. Complete the dialogue.**

Saleswoman: Ticket Office. How [1] .... help you?

Gavin: Hello. [2] .... about tickets for tonight's concert.

Saleswoman: [3] ...., we've only got tickets for Saturday.

Gavin: Oh. How [4] .... they?

Saleswoman: They're £50 each.

Gavin: Oh, That's quite expensive. I need to talk to my friends. Can I [5] .... later?

Saleswoman: Yes, of course.

Gavin: OK. Thanks. Bye.

2 marks per item: ...... / 10 marks

Total marks: ...... / 100

3A Health news

Vocabulary: health problems

1 Write the name of the illness or health problem above each statement. Use the words in the box.

| an allergy   a cold   asthma   chicken pox   malaria |
| flu   hay fever   measles   a nosebleed   tonsillitis |

1 ....
He put a handkerchief to his nose, held his head forward and waited for it to stop.

2 ....
Most children get it when they are young. They get a temperature and horrible, itchy spots.

3 ....
You get red spots all over your body and it can cause serious complications.

4 ....
Mosquitoes carry the parasite that causes this killer disease.

5 ....
My throat was red and infected so the doctor gave me antibiotics.

6 ....
The usual symptoms are a cough, a runny nose and a sore throat. It's not a serious illness and people still go to school and to work.

7 ....
It's most common in springtime when there's a lot of pollen in the air. My friend gets it and her eyes get red and itchy.

8 ....
Sometimes it's really bad. I can't breathe at all and I have to go to hospital.

9 ....
Her temperature was very high and her whole body ached. She spent five days in bed.

10 ....
I can't wear metal jewellery. It gives me a skin rash.

Working with words: noun + noun

2 Complete the paragraph with compound nouns. Use the illustrations to help you.

My day

I'm a champion
¹ .... so I have to train hard every day.

This morning I went running and listened to music on my MP3 player. It was cold and very windy but I didn't get earache because the
² .... from my MP3 player protected my ears.

When I got home, I had an
³ .... and some breakfast and then went to school.

At ⁴ .... I ate sandwiches and some tropical fruit called papaya. My friends all bought
⁵ .... from the school canteen. In the afternoon, I started coughing and developed a rash on my face, so I went to the doctor's. She said it was probably an allergy and gave me some
⁶ .... and some ⁷ ...., which tasted awful! Maybe I'll have burgers and chips in future!

Lily Jones

3 Match the words in each column to form compound nouns.

1	ear	**a**	technology
2	flu	**b**	ache
3	bed	**c**	killers
4	art	**d**	team
5	rugby	**e**	makers
6	head	**f**	room
7	tooth	**g**	story
8	food	**h**	room
9	holiday	**i**	gallery
10	news	**j**	drops
11	music	**k**	virus
12	pain	**l**	ache

4 Complete the dialogues with words in Exercise 3.

1
A: Have you seen today's newspaper? What's the main .... ?

B: It's about the .... It's really bad this year and they still haven't developed a vaccine for it.

2
A: What did the dentist give you for your .... ?

B: She gave me some strong ....

3
A: I've got .... this afternoon. What about you?

B: I'll be in the .... We're practising for the concert.

4
A: There are a lot of .... in town today.

B: Yes. They've come to see the exhibition at the ....

Grammar: present perfect with *yet*, *already* and *just*

5 Complete the sentences with the present perfect and *just*. Use the words in brackets.

1 Please take your shoes off. .... (I / clean / floors)

2 Shhh. .... (the baby / go / to sleep)

3 You look nice. ....? (go / the hairdresser's)

4 I should feel better soon. .... (I / take / a painkiller)

5 Sorry. Mike's not here. .... (he / leave / for work)

6 Would you like some cake? .... (I / make / it)

6 Look at Lily's 'To do' list. Make statements and questions with *already* and *yet*. Use short forms.

TO DO
Saturday morning
put in ear drops ✓
take cough medicine ✓
wash tennis kit ✗
do homework ✗
phone tennis coach ✓
download new songs onto MP3 ✓
go to the supermarket with mum ✗

she / put in / ear drops.
She's already put in her ear drops.

1 she / do / everything on her list / ?
....

2 she / take / cough medicine.
....

3 she / wash / tennis kit / ?
....

4 she / do / her homework.
....

5 she / phone / tennis coach / ?
....

6 she / download / new songs onto her MP3 / ?
....

7 she / go / supermarket with mum.
....

Grammar: *for* and *since*

7 Complete the sentences with *for* or *since*.

1 I haven't been ill .... a long time.

2 There haven't been any new cases of flu .... April.

3 People have used honey to treat a sore throat .... many years.

4 Sue has had a headache .... this morning.

5 The new hospital has been open .... 2009.

6 The doctor is very busy. We've been in the waiting room .... hours.

8 Complete the sentences. Circle the correct option (a, b or c).

1 Have you seen the doctor ....?
a already　　**b** yet　　**c** since

2 I have .... had two of my vaccinations. I've got another one next week.
a already　　**b** yet　　**c** since

3 Jonathan hasn't had a temperature .... last night. I think he can go to school today.
a for　　**b** since　　**c** just

4 I feel awful! I've .... seen a terrible car accident.
a just　　**b** yet　　**c** already

5 My father has stopped smoking. He hasn't had a cigarette .... six months.
a since　　**b** already　　**c** for

Reading

1 You are going to read an interview with Sylwia Gruchała. Put the words into the correct order to make the questions.

1 start / did / when / fencing / you / ?

....

2 any / for / readers / do / have / our / you / advice / ?

....

3 do / you / diet / strict / follow / a / ?

....

4 greatest / been / your / what / far / have / achievements / so / ?

....

5 sports / exercise / do / kinds / do / other / of / what / and / you / ?

....

6 health / any / had / ever / you / problems / have / ?

....

2 Read the interview and match Sylwia's answers (paragraphs a–f) with the questions (1–6) from Exercise 1.

3 Read the interview again. Choose the correct answer (a, b or c).

1 Sylwia Gruchała has won:
  a three World Championships.
  b two Olympic medals.
  c two European Championships.

2 When Sylwia started fencing:
  a she wasn't very good at it.
  b she was a teenager.
  c she didn't enjoy it.

3 When Sylwia isn't training, she:
  a goes running with a club.
  b rides her bicycle near her home.
  c goes walking.

4 Sylwia eats:
  a about five big meals a day.
  b large salads every day.
  c lots of small meals during the day.

5 Sylwia has never:
  a smoked.
  b drunk wine.
  c had an operation.

6 Sylwia believes that people:
  a need to follow their dreams.
  b need to do lots of hard physical exercise.
  c need to eat more pasta and salad.

Olympic fencer

Sylwia Gruchała is an Olympic fencer. We recently spoke to Sylwia about her achievements, her interests and her lifestyle.

a I've won many competitions and championships, including the World Championships in team fencing in 2003 and 2007. I also won the silver medal at the Olympic Games in 2000. As an individual competitor, I've been the European Champion three times, and I won bronze at the Olympic Games in 2004. All of my successes have given me a lot of joy and satisfaction, but the bronze medal at the Olympic Games in Athens, in 2004 is the most important for me.

b I was very young when I started fencing. I was still at primary school. My school didn't do athletics, so I chose fencing instead. I didn't like it very much but my coach saw that I was talented and wanted me to continue. He helped me a lot. I soon started winning competions and began to enjoy fencing.

c My exercise regime is quite hard work. Apart from training, I do a lot of things by myself, such as stretching and running. I also do mental training, which I believe is extremely important. I go skiing a lot in winter — I adore it! I live in a beautiful place with many cycle paths, so I do a lot of cycling. I also like riding my motorbike and swimming.

d I like Mediterranean food, such as pizza, pasta and big salads. However, as a fencer, it's better to follow a diet. I try to eat little and often. I usually have between five and seven small meals a day. It's also good to drink a lot of water, although I sometimes have a glass of wine with my dinner.

e I'm a very healthy person. I've never smoked and I'm strongly against taking any type of drug. I've had problems with my knees in the past but in 2001, I had an operation. I'm very grateful to my surgeon because I have been able to continue

fencing and have achieved many of my sporting ambitions.

f I believe it is important to think positively and to take care of your body. In addition, everyone needs to have goals and find satisfaction in following their dreams.

Listening

4 🔘 **3.1** Listen to a teenager telling his friend about a disabled athlete. Choose the best photo (a or b).

5 Listen again. Are the sentences true or false?

	T	F
1 Scout Bassett was born with only one leg.	☐	☐
2 She had to clean the floors when she was only three.	☐	☐
3 Her first artificial leg was uncomfortable.	☐	☐
4 She has lived in America for two years.	☐	☐
5 She's been running in competitions since she was fourteen years old.	☐	☐
6 Scout hasn't won any big competitions yet.	☐	☐

Working with words: adjective + preposition

6 Complete the sentences from the listening in Exercise 5 with the correct prepositions.

1 I've trained really hard this month and I'm tired .... it.

2 I've had to get up at six o'clock every morning and I'm fed up .... it.

3 I'm really tired and I get annoyed .... everyone.

4 But you're really good .... athletics!

5 When I get nervous .... competitions, I think about Scout.

6 She can be really proud .... herself.

7 Circle the odd one out.

1 Are you *afraid of / frightened of / tired of* heights?

2 I'm really *pleased with / good at / happy with* this picture I've painted.

3 My brother broke my new CD. I'm really *excited about / annoyed with / angry with* him.

4 Kirsten is *bad at / not very good at / not interested in* sport. She enjoys it, but she isn't athletic.

5 Liz didn't study before her exams. Now she feels *nervous about / worried about / scared of* her results.

6 We are very *proud of / ashamed of / pleased with* tonight's show. It was a perfect performance.

8 Complete the second sentence so that it means the same as the first sentence. Use the adjectives in the box with an appropriate preposition.

> confused   ~~fed up~~   good   interested   proud   scared   worried

This book isn't interesting.

I'm *fed up with* this book.

1 I love physics and chemistry!
I'm really .... them.

2 I usually get good grades in science.
I'm .... science.

3 This year I think I did badly in my exams.
I'm .... my results this year.

4 My sister feels frightened when she sees a spider.
My sister is .... spiders.

5 I didn't understand the last two questions.
I was .... the last two questions.

6 My parents were very pleased when I got top marks last year.
My parents were .... me when I got top marks last year.

Grammar: present perfect or past simple

9 Circle the correct option.

1 I *have been / went* to my grandparents' house last Sunday.

2 Lorenzo *has lived / lived* in Britain since he was born.

3 My sister *has gone / went* to Paris. She'll be back next week.

4 My dad *joined / has joined* a gym two weeks ago.

5 My grandmother *had / has had* seven children before she was thirty.

6 You're very late! Where *did you go / have you been*?

Useful expressions

1 **Complete the dialogue with the correct expressions (a–f).**

a Neither did we.
b Me neither!
c Me too!
d So did we!
e I wasn't!
f So were we.

Gail: Hey, Max! Where have you been? You're really brown!

Max: We went to Wales for a family holiday.

Gail: Really? [1] .... We got back yesterday. Which part of Wales did you visit?

Max: We were in North Wales.

Gail: [2] .... But we didn't stay near the beach.

Max: [3] .... We went camping in the mountains and I did loads of outdoor sports, including bungee jumping.

Gail: [4] .... I only did one bungee jump, though. I didn't enjoy it at all!

Max: [5] .... It was too scary.

Gail: And I was cold most of the time, as well.

Max: [6] .... I just wore a T-shirt and shorts all week.

Gail: That explains why you're so brown!

2 **Read the dialogue and choose the correct picture.**

Annie: Have you ever been in hospital?

Naomi: Yes, I was in hospital last summer.

Annie: Really? [1] .... was I. Did you have an operation?

Naomi: No, I didn't.

Annie: [2] .... did I.

Naomi: So why were you there? What happened to you?

Annie: I went to a music festival and became very ill.

Naomi: Me [3] ....! That's amazing. Why were you ill?

Annie: I got wet and caught pneumonia.

Naomi: [4] .... did I! I was outside in the rain all day and in the evening I had a high temperature. I thought it was just a cold. I wasn't worried, though.

Annie: [5] .... was I. I had a sore throat and a headache, too. So I took a painkiller and got into my sleeping bag inside the tent.

Naomi: Yeah. Me [6] .... Then, at night, I felt really terrible. Actually, I have never felt so awful in my life!

Annie: [7] .... have I! And my friends were really worried about me. In the end they called an ambulance and it took me to the hospital in the next town.

3 **Complete the dialogue in Exercise 2 with *neither, so* or *too*.**

4 **Complete the dialogue with expressions from Exercises 1 and 2.**

Hannah: I love outdoor sports.

Mike: Really? [1] ....!

Hannah: Have you ever been mountain climbing?

Mike: Yes, I have. My family are all good at climbing. Last year, we went climbing in America.

Hannah: [2] .... We went to Alaska, but I didn't go ice-climbing.

Mike: I did! I loved it! It was fantastic!

Hannah: Have you ever had a climbing accident?

Mike: Yes, I broke my leg in America.

Hannah: [3] ....! I broke it in Alaska and had to stay in hospital.

Mike: We didn't go home for three weeks!

Hannah: [4] .... I was really fed up and bored.

Mike: Yeah. [5] ....!

5 🔘 **3.2** **Listen and check your answers to Exercise 4.**

Pronunciation: vowel sounds /æ/ and /ʌ/ in irregular verbs

6 🔘 **3.3** **Listen and circle the sound you hear.**

1 He *rang* / *'s rung* his friend on his mobile phone.

2 She *swam* / *'s swum* across the lake.

3 It *'s begun* / *began* to rain.

4 Who *'s sung* / *sang* in the choir?

5 He *'s run* / *ran* in many competitions.

Writing: an article

7 Read Georgina's email to an online teen magazine. Choose the correct answer (a, b or c).

Georgina is worried about Michelle because:

a they aren't friends anymore.

b she's become thin and unhappy.

c she never does her homework.

I'm really worried about my best friend, Michelle. She's completely changed recently. Before, she was really cheerful and happy, but now she seems sad. In the past, we talked a lot about everything, but we haven't had a good conversation for months. However, the worst thing is that she's getting really thin and she hasn't got any energy. She has got bad marks in school this term, too. Although she eats at lunchtime, she always leaves a lot of food on her plate. I have never seen her eat anything at break-time. I've been to her house for tea a few times. Even though Michelle eats her meal, she takes a long time to finish it. She usually finishes her food alone, while everyone else is watching television in the living room. What should I do? Should I talk to her parents?
Georgina

8 Match Georgina's letter with the best reply (a, b or c).

a Your friend needs to do more sport. She isn't very healthy and this is why she doesn't eat much. You should take her running or swimming. Then you should go to a fast food restaurant and have a hamburger and chips. I'm sure she will enjoy it.

b Your friend probably has a problem that she is keeping secret. Maybe she has problems at home or with a boyfriend. You should talk to her. Show that you are interested in her. You should also tell her parents that she doesn't eat at school. Perhaps she doesn't like school meals.

c Your friend has a serious eating disorder and she needs help. However, it's not easy to help someone like her. You need to be very careful. You shouldn't try to talk to her yourself – she needs expert help. I think you should talk to your teacher. He or she will know what to do.

9 Choose the correct expression or expressions in each sentence.

1 The friends talked a lot in the past. *Although / Even though / However*, it's several months since they last had a good conversation.

2 *Although / Even though / However* Michelle buys food at lunchtime, she always leaves a lot on her plate.

3 At home Michelle always eats her evening meal. *Although / Even though / However*, she takes a long time to finish it.

4 Georgina wants to help Michelle, *although / even though / however* it's not easy to help somebody with an eating disorder.

5 *Although / Even though / However* Georgina wants to talk to Michelle about her problem, she is not sure that this is the best thing to do.

10 Put the phrases (a–f) in the correct order in the sentences (1–6) to complete the story.

1 I'm really worried about my little brother...

2 They laugh at him in the playground...

3 Although they call him horrible names...

4 Mum gives him dinner money every morning...

5 Although I've asked him about the boys many times ...

6 I don't know what to do. ...

a but I think the bullies steal it – he doesn't buy food at lunchtime.

b because I think some older boys are bullying him.

c and push him in the corridors.

d I've never seen him cry.

e Should I talk to his teacher?

f he won't ever talk to me about them.

11 Write a letter to a problem page about your brother. Use the ideas in Exercise 10. Add *although, even though* and *however*. Use Georgina's letter in Exercise 7 to help you.

Reading

1 **Read the text and match the correct headings (a–d) with each section (1–3). There is one extra heading.**

a The cost of smoking

b Why smoking is an addiction

c Diseases related to smoking

d The number of people who give up smoking

Stop Smoking!

1

Smoking is bad for your health. Everybody knows that. However, millions of people continue to smoke all over the world. In the USA, about 19.2 million smokers try to give up cigarettes once a year, but only five percent of them stay tobacco free for more than three months. The other ninety-five per cent are unsuccessful and start smoking again after a few days.

2

Cigarettes contain a drug called nicotine, which is very addictive. A study of teenagers showed that they became addicted just two days after smoking their first cigarette. When smokers try to stop smoking, they feel unhappy and in a bad mood. Some people also feel physically ill. They 'need' a cigarette to feel normal again.

3

It is important to help smokers to give up. Smoking can cause heart disease and lung cancer as well as other diseases. People who stop smoking feel healthier very quickly. After one year, the risk of heart disease is cut by fifty percent. After ten years, the risk of lung cancer is also cut by half.

2 **Complete the gapped text with the correct form of the words in the box.**

be	good	have got

Dear Grandma,

We're sorry to hear that you ¹ .... ill for the last few weeks. We hope that you are feeling ² .... now. Have you had a lot of visitors? We hope you ³ .... lots of flowers and fruit! Mum says we can come next weekend. We'll bring you a nice present! See you soon.

Lots of love,

Hannah and Ryan

3 **Complete the gapped text with the correct form of the words in the box.**

go	take	tooth

Hi Mum,

I ¹ .... to the dentist on the bus. One of my ² .... started hurting this afternoon. I ³ .... some painkillers when I got home from school, but they didn't work. Can you come and pick me up when I finish at the dentist?

Max

P.S. I'll phone you on my mobile.

Word list | Unit 3

abroad (adv)	....
according to (adv)	....
achieve (v)	....
achievement (n)	....
addiction (n)	....
addictive (n)	....
adore (v)	....
adult (n)	....
affect (v)	....
announce (v)	....
artificial (adj)	....
ash (n)	....
bad habit (n phr)	....
fed up (adj)	....
blood cell (n)	....
bottom (n)	....
breathe (v)	....
bronchitis (n)	....
cancer (n)	....
carbon dioxide (n)	....
cardboard (n)	....
championship (n)	....
chicken pox (n)	....
coach (n)	....
competitor (n)	....
cone (n)	....
confident (adj)	....
cough (n)	....
crisps (n)	....
cure (n)	....
cycle path (n)	....
deliberately (adv)	....
digest (v)	....
disorder (n)	....
donation (n)	....
donor (n)	....
doughnut (n)	....
drug (n)	....
earpiece (n)	....
entertaining (adj)	....
epilepsy (n)	....

fencer (n)	....
fizzy drink (n)	....
flame (n)	....
get angry with (phr)	....
get sunburnt (phr)	....
give up (phr v)	....
goal (n)	....
goat (n)	....
grade (n)	....
grateful (adj)	....
handkerchief (n)	....
hay fever (n)	....
hepatitis (n)	....
honey (n)	....
horizontal (adj)	....
identify (v)	....
illness (n)	....
increase (v)	....
insect-repellent (n)	....
itchy (adj)	....
junk food (n phr)	....
launch (v)	....
lift up (phr v)	....
liquid (n)	....
limit (v)	....
lose weight (phr)	....
lung (n)	....
measles (n)	....
medicine (n)	....
mood (n)	....
mosquito (n)	....
mystery (n)	....
net (n)	....
nosebleed (n)	....
oxygen (n)	....
painkiller (n)	....
parasite (n)	....
perform (v)	....
plague (n)	....
poison (n)	....
pollen (n)	....

polluted (adj)	....
pollution (n)	....
properly (adv)	....
pyromaniac (n)	....
raft (n)	....
raise money (phr)	....
rash (n)	....
recover (v)	....
regime (n)	....
resistant (adj)	....
rucksack (n)	....
scuba-diving (n)	....
several (pron)	....
solid (adj)	....
sting (n)	....
sunstroke (n)	....
surgeon (n)	....
surround (v)	....
tennis kit (n)	....
thick (adj)	....
threat (n)	....
thunderstorm (n)	....
tobacco (n)	....
tonsillitis (n)	....
typhoid (n)	....
vaccination (n)	....
vegetation (n)	....

U3 Reading Explorer

beak (n)	....
bloodsucker (n)	....
leech (n)	....
moth (n)	....
needle (n)	....
prey on (v)	....
sharp (adj)	....
spoonful (n)	....
suck (v)	....
swelling (n)	....
treat (n)	....
tick (n)	....
wound (n)	....

Grammar Practice Unit 3

present perfect with *yet, already* and *just*

We use *yet* in questions and negative sentences; it goes at the end of the sentence.
– *Have you watched that new DVD **yet**?*
– *No, I haven't watched it **yet**.*

We use *already* in affirmative sentences; it usually goes between *have/has* and the main verb.
*I've **already** watched that DVD.*

We use *just* to show that something happened a very short time ago.
*I've **just** put the DVD in the player!*

1 Put the words into the correct order to make sentences and questions.

you / the doctor / yet / have / to see / been / ?
Have you been to see the doctor yet?

1 already / has / his typhoid injection / Lee / had / .
....

2 has / Jack / yet / his science project / finished / ?
....

3 Lauren / just / has / to Aneta / sent / a text message / .
....

4 had / Karen / already / twice this winter / flu / has / .
....

5 a cure / yet / found / haven't / for this disease / scientists / .
....

6 just / I / a painkiller / taken / have / for my headache / .
....

2 Write sentences and questions in the present perfect. Use the words in brackets.

the nurse / take / his temperature / . (**just**)
The nurse has just taken his temperature.

1 Simon / not tell / his parents the news / . (**yet**)
....

2 We / pack / our suitcases for the trip / . (**already**)
....

3 Daisy / begin / studying for the test / ? (**yet**)
....

4 Lee / leave / Aneta's house / . (**just**)
....

5 Wow – it / start / snowing / ! (**just**)
....

6 I / not have / dinner / . (**yet**)
....

present perfect with *for* and *since*

We use *for* to talk about duration.
*Pam has been a nurse **for** three years.*
We use *since* to talk about when a state or situation started.
*We've lived in this house **since** 2005.*

3 Complete the sentences with *for* or *since*.

I've been a student at this school *for* three years.

1 Josie's really healthy – she hasn't been sick ...... at least two years.
2 Jack and Lauren have been friends ...... they were very young.
3 My grandmother has been ill ...... last week.
4 Where's Ben? I haven't seen him ...... days.
5 Zinah has made lots of friends ...... she arrived in Cambridge.

present perfect and past simple

We use the **present perfect** to talk about:
• a state that continues up to the present
• an action that has been repeated a number of times and may be repeated again in the future

We use the **past simple** to talk about a completed action in the past. We use this when:
• we say when the action happened
• the period of time in which it happened does not continue up to the present

4 Complete the sentences with the present perfect or past simple form of the verbs.

Sandra *went* (go) to see the doctor this morning.

1 Lauren's cousin ...... (come) to stay with her last month.
2 Lee ...... (not have) an email from his brother since October.
3 Mike ...... (not do) well in his maths test yesterday.
4 Aneta ...... (not see) her cousins for two years.
5 Matt ...... (break) his leg in the rugby match on Saturday.

So / Neither + auxiliary verb or be + subject

We use *so* to agree with an affirmative statement, and *neither* to agree with a negative statement.

The pattern is *So / Neither + modal / auxiliary / be + subject*.

*Jack **can** play the violin. So **can** Lee.*

*She **doesn't** like sports. Neither **does** he.*

If the statement doesn't have a modal, auxiliary or *be*, we use *do(n't)/does(n't)* or *did(n't)*.

Another way to agree with another person's statement is to use **Me too** and **Me neither**.

A: I was really bored.   *B: **Me too.***

A: I haven't had lunch yet.   *B: **Me neither.***

When someone makes a statement about their feelings etc, another person might disagree.
In this case, we can use **subject + modal / auxiliary / be**.

A: I was really bored.   *B: **I wasn't.***

A: I haven't had lunch yet.   *B: **I have.***

5 **Match statements 1–6 with responses a–g.**

I've been to America. ..c..   **a** Me too.

1 Ann can't speak German. ....   **b** I am.

2 Tom doesn't like sports. ....   **c** So have I.

3 Jack plays the violin. ....   **d** Neither can I.

4 Matt went to France. ....   **e** Me neither.

5 They aren't watching TV. ....   **f** Neither was I.

6 Dan wasn't at school. ....   **g** I didn't.

6 **Write responses agreeing (✓) or disagreeing (✗) with the statements.**

I've been to America. (✗) ..I haven't..

1 Cathy has never had measles. (✓) ......

2 Aneta loves reading detective stories. (✗) ......

3 Lee is going to China at Christmas. (✗) ......

4 We'll be on holiday next week. (✓) ......

5 I didn't enjoy that movie. (✗) ......

Although, Even though, However

Although and *even though* show that the one action, etc is the opposite of what we would expect to follow another.

Although Lee was ill, he went to the party.

Lee went to school, even though he was ill.

However begins a sentence about the opposite action/etc.

*I can play the guitar. **However**, I can't play the piano.*

7 **Choose the correct words.**

Although / ~~However~~ it was hot, he was wearing a coat.

1 I expected to get here at six o'clock. *Even though / However,* the train was late.

2 *Even though / However* he was tired, he finished his homework.

3 Jack didn't eat lunch *although / however* he was hungry.

4 She took a painkiller half an hour ago. *Even though / However,* she has still got a headache.

8 **Write the sentences using the linking words.**

She had a temperature. She didn't stay in bed. (**even though**)

Even though she had a temperature, she didn't stay in bed.

1 It was very cold. Jack and Lauren still played tennis. (**however**)

....

2 I didn't like the CD much. I decided to buy it. (**although**)

....

3 She doesn't do well at school. She's very clever. (**even though**)

....

4 He's going on holiday tomorrow. He hasn't packed his suitcase yet. (**although**)

....

5 Mum wants to buy a new car. Dad doesn't agree. (**however**)

....

4A The environment

Vocabulary: natural disasters

1 Complete the table with the words in the box.

~~avalanche~~	~~drought~~	~~earthquake~~	flood
hurricane	lightning	storm	tornado
tsunami	volcano	wildfire	

Caused by movement of land (or under the earth)	Extreme weather or the result of extreme weather	Sometimes caused by people
earthquake	drought	avalanche
....	....	....
....	....	
....	....	
	....	
	....	

2 Answer the questions.

1 Which two natural disasters are caused by too much rain?

2 What happens if there has been no rain for a long period of time?

3 What is the result of negative electric charges in the sky?

4 What spreads quickly across dry land?

5 What produces lava and ash?

6 Which natural disaster is a danger to skiers and mountain climbers?

Working with words: adjective + noun

3 Complete the questions and answers with the adjectives in the box.

| bad | best | free | healthy | junk | mobile |
| video | violent | volcanic | wild | | |

1 Q: What does a .... lifestyle involve?

 A: You should do some exercise in your .... time, and you shouldn't eat .... food.

2 Q: What causes a .... eruption?

 A: It is usually the result of a .... movement inside the earth.

3 Q: Yasmina's photos of .... animals are fantastic. What camera did she use?

 A: I think she used the .... camera on her .... phone.

4 Q: Why is Maxine in a .... mood?

 A: She's had an argument with her .... friend.

4 Complete the sentences with a word from each box.

bad	~~global~~	human
industrial	living	
natural	tropical	

activity	age	disaster
disease	habit	thing
~~warming~~		

Earth is getting hotter because of *global warming*.

1 A virus is alive. It's a ....

2 Smoking is a very ....

3 A tsunami is a ....

4 Typhoid and malaria are two types of ....

5 A lot of factories and machines were built during the ....

6 The pollution of seas and rivers is caused by ....

Grammar: the present simple passive

5 Circle the correct option.

1 Many countries *are recycled / recycle* plastic.

2 Glass *is made / makes* from sand.

3 Indonesia *is often affected / often affects* by tsunamis.

4 Which country *is produced / produces* the most oil?

5 How many volcanoes *erupt / are erupted* every year?

6 Damage *is caused / causes* by earthquakes.

6 Complete the text. Write the present simple passive form of the verbs in brackets.

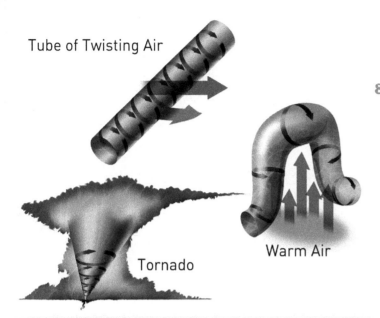

Tube of Twisting Air

Tornado

Warm Air

Tornadoes

In spring and early summer, America ¹ .... (hit) by many violent thunderstorms. They ² ....
(cause) when cool, dry air from Canada meets warm air from Mexico. An area called 'Tornado Alley' in the Midwest, ³.................. (affect) every year by the worst tornadoes in America. Tornadoes ⁴ .... (form) at the bottom of huge thunderclouds. This happens when a slow wind ⁵ .... (twist) round by faster air above it and becomes a horizontal tube of twisting air. Then more warm air comes up from the ground and starts to lift up part of this tube of air to form a loop. When one end of the loop reaches the ground, a tornado ⁶ ....
(create). As the twisting column of air travels across the ground, many trees and buildings ⁷ .... (destroy).

7 Put the words in the correct order to make sentences.

1 was / in / The / recorded / 1917. / tornado / longest

....

2 ruined / an / San Francisco / was / by / in / earthquake / 1906

....

3 150,000 / killed / by / were / 2004. / a / Sri Lankan people / tsunami / in

....

4 ago. / house / Our / hit / lightning / was / two / by / years

....

5 wildfires / last / by / Many / were / of / forests / destroyed / year.

....

6 and / were / injured / storm. / last / week's / people / in / animals / Both

....

8 Write questions for the sentences in Exercise 7. Use the prompts to help you.

1 When / longest tornado / record

....?

2 Which city / ruin / earthquake / 1906

....?

3 How many Sri Lankan people / kill / tsunami / 2004

....?

4 When / your house / hit / lightning

....?

5 What / destroy / wildfires / last year

....?

6 Who / injure / last week's storm

....?

9 Complete the text. Write the correct passive or active form of the verbs in brackets.

Fire!

Most fires ¹ .... (start) by people. Sometimes they ² .... (happen) accidentally. A common cause of wildfires are cigarettes that ³ .... (throw) on the ground. Another cause is when people ⁴ ....
(lose) control of cooking fires. However, some people, called pyromaniacs, are fascinated by fire and deliberately ⁵ .... (start) fires.
In 1666, the city of London ⁶ .... (destroy) by a fire. All the buildings on one side of the river Thames ⁷ .... (burn) to the ground, and thousands of people ⁸ .... (die). Luckily, it also ⁹ ....
(kill) all the rats. This ¹⁰ .... (stop) the spread of a terrible disease, called the Black Plague. Nobody really knows what the Great Fire of London ¹¹.................. (cause) by, but one story is that it ¹² .... (begin) in a bakery.

4B Wild animals

Reading

1 Look at the photos. Tick (✓) the things you can see.

buildings ☐   canoes ☐   flames ☐
mountain ☐   raft ☐   river ☐
smoke ☐   tent ☐   trees ☐

2 Read the story. Choose the best summary of the text.

a A small town was destroyed by fire and many people escaped down the river on rafts.

b Five families were camping near a river when a wildfire burned down their campsite.

c A group of adults and children rowed for two days to escape a burning river.

Escape down the river of fire

Kyle Haynam, 16, and Scotty Craighead, 11, were on a rafting trip with five other children and twenty-three adults. They were rowing down the Salmon River in Idaho, when they saw smoke coming from a mountain in the distance. When they reached camp in the afternoon, they could see flames on the other side of the river. The flames were as high as a three-storey building. The fire was still two miles away, so nobody was worried. Then, suddenly, the wind changed direction and the fire was pushed closer. Everyone was surprised but nobody was frightened. After all, a fire couldn't jump the river ... or could it?

That evening, the wind changed again and burning vegetation was thrown across the river. Kyle and his group were suddenly surrounded by a forest fire. They were trapped! There was only one way to escape. They had to keep rowing to the next campsite. It was very hot and the thick smoke hurt their eyes, so they put wet towels over their faces. When they reached the next campsite, they found it was burned to the ground. The fire on the campsite was out, so it was safe to stay there. However, the mountain above was still on fire and thick smoke filled the air. That night, they slept with wet towels over their faces. 'It was difficult to breathe through the smoke, but it was also difficult to breathe through the towel,' Kyle says.

When they woke early the next morning, it was very cold. The sun was covered by the ash and they couldn't even see the river through the thick smoke. Kyle and his friends were scared. The fire was getting nearer and nearer. 'We were rowing hard and fast because we didn't want to be in the smoke another day,' says Scotty. At five o'clock in the afternoon, they finally reached the river's end. Luckily, everyone on the river that day got back safely, but Kyle's group were the last group to escape from the fire.

3 Read the story again and answer the questions. Choose the correct answer (a, b or c).

1 Where were Kyle and Scotty doing when they saw smoke in the distance?

  a They were at a campsite in the mountains.

  b They were on a raft on the river.

  c They were standing by the river.

2 How did the group of rafters feel when the wind changed and the fire got nearer?

  a They felt scared.

  b They were angry.

  c They were surprised.

3 How did the fire cross the river?

  a A burning tree fell in the water.

  b Burning branches and leaves were blown across the river by the wind.

  c The flames were so big that they could reach the other side of the river.

4 What did the group do at the next campsite?

  a They spent the night there.

  b They left quickly because it was on fire.

  c They slept on the raft next to the campsite.

5 Why was everybody very cold the next morning?

  a Because their clothes were wet.

  b Because the sun didn't rise.

  c Because they couldn't feel the sun through all the ash.

6 Why did Kyle feel scared on the last day?

  a Because they couldn't see where they were going.

  b Because the adults were rowing very fast.

  c Because the fire was getting nearer.

Listening

4  **4.1** Listen to the interview and choose the correct answer (a, b or c).

The man is talking about:

a what causes a tsunami.

b how people escaped from a tsunami.

c how animals survive tsunamis.

5 Listen again. Are the sentences true or false?

		T	F
1	Mr Patel was in Sri Lanka when the tsunami hit.	☐	☐
2	Before the tsunami hit, many animals ran away from the coast.	☐	☐
3	Only wild animals can feel vibrations before an earthquake.	☐	☐
4	About 150,000 animals died in the tsunami.	☐	☐
5	Mr Patel didn't see any dead animals on the beach at Patanangala.	☐	☐
6	Experts believe that, in the past, humans had the ability to sense danger.	☐	☐
7	Mr Patel's life was saved by two dogs.	☐	☐

Grammar: quantifiers + nouns

6 Circle the correct option.

1 *Much / Many* animals survived the 2004 tsunami.

2 There are *few / little* wild otters left in Europe.

3 Is there *much / many* pollution in Alaska?

4 How *many / much* bears did you see in Canada?

5 I found very *little / few* information about wild horses in the library.

6 There was too *little / much* food and people were still hungry.

7 Complete the sentences with the words in the box.

> lot (x2)   lots   most   many   much

1 There were a .... of deer in the park.

2 Not .... people survived the Black Plague.

3 The park ranger gave us .... of information.

4 I ate a .... of food at the party.

5 .... owls only hunt at night, although a few also hunt in the early evening.

6 How .... of London burned down in the Great Fire of 1666?

8 Complete the text with *few, little, lots, many, much* or *most*.

Fact file: the grey wolf

Grey wolves are the largest members of the dog family. [1] .... adult wolves weigh between 27 and 60 kilos.

Diet

Grey wolves have huge appetites. They eat [2] .... of food and can digest up to 80 kilos of meat in one meal! Their diet mainly consists of large animals, such as deer, bison and mountain goat.

Character

The story of the big, bad wolf is very popular, and people believe that wolves are dangerous, aggressive animals. But how [3] .... of this is true? [4] .... wolves are usually quiet and shy. There is very [5] .... evidence to suggest that wolves are a threat to humans. In fact, very [6] .... wolves ever attack people and, in North America, no healthy wolf has ever eaten a human.

Protection

In the past, wolves were hunted all over the world. Until recently, there were not [7] .... grey wolves left in the wild. Today, they are a protected species and the number of wolves in the wild is growing.

Useful expressions

1 Match the beginnings of the useful expressions (1–9) with the endings (a–i).

1 What do you	**a** much about them.
2 I can tell you	**b** no idea.
3 I don't know	**c** I'm sure.
4 I have	**d** possible?
5 That's	**e** a lot about wild horses.
6 I don't	**f** know about wild animals?
7 Are	**g** true.
8 Yes,	**h** you sure?
9 Is that	**i** think so.

2 Complete the dialogue with the expressions from Exercise 1.

Carla: Hi Jake. How's the project going?

Jake: Not very well, I'm afraid. I need some help. ¹ ....?

Carla: Well, I don't know much about wild animals in general, but ² ....

Jake: Hey. That's a good idea for a topic. There are lots of wild horses in America, aren't there?

Carla: Yes. ³ .... They're called Mustangs. But there's only one true wild horse. It is called Przewalski's horse and it is found only in Mongolia.

Jake: Really? ⁴ ....?

Carla: ⁵ .... They were nearly extinct a few years ago. And they're still endangered.

Jake: What about other wild horses?

Carla: Well. There are wild horses in Argentina and there's the Australian Brumby.

Jake: Is the Australian Brumby an endangered species?

Carla: ⁶ .... – I think there are still quite a lot of Australian brumbics in the wild. But I think Argentinian wild horses are endangered.

Jake: OK, that's really useful. Thanks for your help.

Carla: No problem. By the way, can you help me with my maths homework?

3 Choose the correct response (a, b or c).

1 What do you know about volcanoes?
   a I don't think so.
   b Yes, I'm sure.
   c I don't know anything about them.

2 Is the beaver an endangered species?
   a I have no idea.
   b Are you sure?
   c That's true.

3 Is pollution today's biggest environmental problem?
   a I can tell you a lot about it.
   b Is that possible?
   c I don't think so.

4 Recycling is very important.
   a That's true.
   b I have no idea.
   c Yes, I'm sure.

5 The school trip is next week.
   a I can tell you a lot about it.
   b Are you sure?
   c I have no idea.

6 If they have fresh water, most humans can survive without food for more than a month.
   a Yes, I'm sure.
   b I have no idea.
   c Is that possible?

4 Complete the dialogue. Use the useful expressions from Exercise 1 and Exercise 3 to help you.

Jake: Are you going on the school trip?

Holly: What trip? Our teacher hasn't given us the information yet, so I don't ¹ .... about it.

Jake: Well, my form teacher's organising the trip, so I can ² .... about it.

Holly: OK, so where's the trip to?

Jake: We're going to visit a safari park in the South of France.

Holly: In France? Really? Is ³ ....? It's so far away.

Jake: Of course it's possible! There are lots of flights and the park is next to the airport.

Holly: So what kinds of animals can we see?

Jake: All kinds – lions, tigers, giraffes, hippos.

Holly: Lions and tigers? Are ⁴ ....?

Jake: Yes, ⁵ .... We'll be with a ranger in the park, so we'll be safe.

Holly: It sounds great. But how much does it cost?

Jake: I have ⁶ .... but Mr Smith is going to send a letter out about it.

Pronunciation: the letter 'o' and the vowel sounds /ʊ/, /uː/ and /ʌ/

5 Say the words and circle the odd one out.

1	blood	flood	shoot
2	good	cook	come
3	move	book	shoot
4	put	foot	boot
5	wolf	but	blood
6	push	come	took

6 ⊙ **4.2** Listen and check your answers to Exercise 5.

Writing: a description of a place

7 Holly and Jake have written articles about local places for their school magazine. Read Holly's article. Which place has she written about?

a her town

b her garden

c her local park

8 Read the article again and circle the correct option in each sentence.

9 Complete Jake's article with the linking words in the box.

> also   also   for example   including   such as   too

I live in a big city which is full of cars and buildings and lots of noise. However, there are ¹ .... quiet, peaceful places, ² .... the park and the river.

The park is in the centre of the city. It is full of big trees, lots of grass and there is also quite a lot of wildlife ³ .... You can often see rabbits and squirrels running across the grass. In the middle of the park, there is a small lake. Many different birds visit the lake, especially in winter.

The river is ⁴ .... home to a lot of wildlife, ⁵ .... rare plants and water mammals, such as otters. Large birds often build nests near the river, ⁶ ...., one year I saw a stork's nest high up in a tree, and last year I think I saw an eagle!

Jake

10 Choose a place you find interesting. Write two or three paragraphs about the place and the wildlife you can see there. Use Holly and Jake's articles to help you. Include the linking words from Exercise 9.

An interesting place

Even if you live in a big city, you don't need to go to special places, ¹ *such as / including* parks and zoos to find wildlife. Just take a look in your garden! You will have to sit quietly for a while and you will ² *also / too* need to be patient. But you may be surprised by what you see.

My own small back garden is a very interesting place. It's especially full of life at this time of year. ³ *For example / such as*, if you sit and watch for just a few minutes, it's amazing to see just how many bees, butterflies, ants and other insects pass by. Many different birds visit the garden, ⁴ *including / also* owls. They sit in the big tree at the bottom of the garden and hoot loudly. In fact, the garden is busier at night than during the day. You can see families of hedgehogs, and you can ⁵ *too / also* see bats flying around. But the most exciting thing for me is when we get a visit from the town fox. We often hear him first, because he goes into the rubbish bins looking for food. We sometimes see him ⁶ *also / too*, but usually we only see his beautiful, red tail disappearing over the garden wall!

Holly

Reading

1 Read the text and match the sentences (a–d) with the gaps (1–3). There is one extra sentence.

Local disasters

Our area is often hit by big storms. In 2008, we had the worst storm for many years. ¹ .... Early this year, the whole town was completely flooded. The water was as high as a two-storey building. ² .... Others were rescued from their rooftops by helicopter. ³ .... Today, a lot of families still haven't returned to their homes.

a They spent the following few days in schools in the next town.

b Some people escaped on rafts made from bits of furniture.

c It reached the tops of the houses.

d Many buildings were damaged by the strong winds.

2 Read the text and match the sentences (a–d) with the gaps (1–3). There is one extra sentence.

Przewalski's horse

Przewalski's horses are the last truly wild horses that exist today. ¹ .... This is because their habitat is being destroyed and they are killed by hunters. ² .... Until recently, there were about 1,500 horses in zoos and almost none in the wild. However, conservationists are now beginning to release horses back into their natural habitats. ³ ....

a Extreme weather conditions also make it more difficult for them to survive in the wild.

b The Mongolian name for these horses is 'takhi,' which means 'spirit'.

c Today, you can see them in the wild again in national parks in Mongolia.

d However, they are a critically endangered species.

3 Read the text and choose the correct option (a, b or c).

The ¹ .... in this photo lives in a zoo. It is swimming in a big tank of water which is made of glass. Three girls are ² .... next to the glass. The polar bear is interested in the girls and has swum over to ³ .... at them. It is looking at the girl on the left. The bear's ⁴ .... is almost touching the glass. The photograph ⁵ .... taken by the girls' father.

1 a brown bear	**b** polar bear	**c** panda
2 a sitting	**b** looking	**c** standing
3 a look	**b** see	**c** meet
4 a tail	**b** leg	**c** face
5 a was	**b** has	**c** is

accommodation (n)	....	flood (n)	....
ankle (n)	....	forest (n)	....
available (adj)	....	fox (n)	....
avalanche (n)	....	fuel (n)	....
ban (v)	....	global warming (n)	....
bat (n)	....	habitat (n)	....
bear (n)	....	headdress (n)	....
beaver (n)	....	hedgehog (n)	....
bell (n)	....	hill walking (n)	....
bison (n)	....	hoot (v)	....
boar (n)	....	huge (adj)	....
carbon footprint (n phr)	....	hunt (v)	....
carer (n)	....	impact (n)	....
cave (n)	....	importance (n)	....
chalet (n)	....	improve (v)	....
confirm (v)	....	industrial (adj)	....
conservationist (n)	....	industrial waste (n)	....
content (adj)	....	instead (adv)	....
create (v)	....	lake (n)	....
cross (v)	....	lazy (adj)	....
dam (n)	....	lightning (n)	....
data (n)	....	limestone (n)	....
declare (v)	....	lynx (n)	....
deer (n)	....	magnificent (adj)	....
deforestation (n)	....	melt (v)	....
desert (n)	....	mountainous (adj)	....
destroy (v)	....	movement (n)	....
disappear (v)	....	mudslide (n)	....
disaster (n)	....	nest (n)	....
domestic (adj)	....	objective (n)	....
drought (n)	....	occur (v)	....
dump (v)	....	on the other hand (phr)	....
eagle (n)	....	otter (n)	....
Earth's cr'ust (n)	....	owl (n)	....
earthquake (n)	....	paddle (v)	....
endangered species (n)	....	pastimes (n)	....
enormous (adj)	....	patient (adj)	....
environment (n)	....	predator (n)	....
equator (n)	....	prisoner (n)	....
equipment (n)	....	protected (adj)	....
erupt (v)	....	pure-bred (adj)	....
event (n)	....	rare (adj)	....
extinct (adj)	....	reason (n)	....
farmland (n)	....	recycle (v)	....
feed (v)	....	reintroduce (v)	....
		relationship (n)	....

release (v)	....
relevant (adj)	....
remote (adj)	....
rescue (v)	....
rock (n)	....
rooftop (n)	....
rubbish tip (n)	....
sacred (adj)	....
sailing (n)	....
scenery (n)	....
shelter (n)	....
shot (v) shoot – shot – shot	....
smoke (n)	....
solar power (n)	....
source (n)	....
squirrel (n)	....
stork (n)	....
storm (n)	....
strength (n)	....
support (v)	....
tank (n)	....
threaten (v)	....
throw away (phr v)	....
tiny (adj)	....
track (v)	....
trout fishing (n)	....
unfamiliar (adj)	....
urban development (n)	....
valley (n)	....
volunteer (n)	....
waste (n)	....
wildfire (n)	....
wolf (n)	....

U4 Reading Explorer

aggressive (adj)	....
charm (v)	....
contaminate (v)	....
dorsal fin (n)	....
estuary (n)	....
extinct flipper (n)	....
forehead (n)	....
glow (v)	....
marine (adj)	....
scar (n)	....
toxic waste (n)	....

passive: present simple, past simple

In active voice, the subject of the sentence is the person/group/thing that does or causes the action. When we use the **passive**, the object of a sentence in active voice becomes the subject of the sentence in the passive.

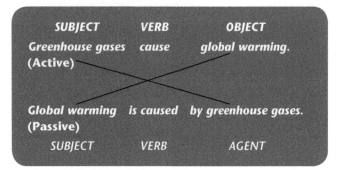

SUBJECT	VERB	OBJECT
Greenhouse gases (Active)	cause	global warming.

Global warming (Passive)	is caused	by greenhouse gases.
SUBJECT	VERB	AGENT

We form the passive with *be* + **past participle** of the verb in the active sentence.

*The earthquake **caused** enormous damage.*
(past simple)

*Enormous damage **was caused** by the earthquake.*

We form the negative with ***isn't/aren't*** + **past participle** in the present simple, and ***wasn't/weren't*** + **past participle** in the past simple.

*The hurricane **isn't expected** to reach the island until tomorrow.*

We use the passive when we want to emphasise the action. If we want to say who/what does the action (the 'agent'), we use *by*.

*Rainforest areas **are cleared** by people for use as farmland.*

1 Complete the sentences with the present simple passive form of the verbs in brackets.

Sandra *went* (**go**) to see the doctor this morning.

1 About 60% of the waste in this city ...... (**recycle**).

2 I ...... (**surprise**) that some people don't care about pollution.

3 Our water supply ...... (**test**) regularly to make sure it's safe.

4 All of us ...... (**affect**) by global climate change.

5 This company's products ...... (**make**) from 100% recycled materials.

6 Wind power ...... (**used**) in several countries nowadays.

2 Complete the short text with the past simple passive form of the verbs.

On 12 January 2010, Haiti *was hit* (hit) by a massive earthquake measuring 7.0 on the Richter scale. Over 200,000 people [1] ...... (kill) in the earthquake, another 300,000 [2] ...... (injure) and about a million people [3] ...... (leave) homeless. Most buildings in the capital, Port au Prince, [4] ...... (destroy) and many people [5] ...... (trap) inside the fallen buildings. The damage [6] ...... (make) worse by the fact that the houses [7] ...... (not build) to withstand a major earthquake. Almost as soon as the disaster [8] ...... (report), rescue workers and equipment [9] ...... (send) by several countries, and aid programmes [10] ...... (organise) to provide food, shelter and medical care.

3 Write the sentences in the passive.

Hunters kill elephants.
Elephants are killed by hunters.

1 Seismographs measure earthquakes.

....

2 A meteor impact killed most of the world's dinosaurs.

....

3 Urban development threatens various wildlife habitats.

....

4 More than 50 years ago, some scientists predicted global warming.

....

5 Humans cause many of the world's environmental problems.

....

We form questions in the passive by putting ***Is/Are*** or ***Was/Were*** before the subject, and then the past participle of the main verb.

***Was** this building **designed** to withstand an earthquake?*

We can use **question words** such as ***What, Why, Where, How***, etc. to ask for extra information rather than a simple 'Yes' or 'No' answer.

***How many** rainforest trees **are cut down** every day?*

4 Rewrite the sentences as questions in the passive, using the question words given.

Hunters kill elephants <u>for their tusks</u>.
Why *are elephants killed by hunters*?

1 They discovered a new species of elephant <u>in 2001</u>.
When .... ?

2 <u>Greenhouse gases</u> cause global warming.
What .... ?

3 They protect some species <u>by banning hunting</u>.
How .... ?

4 <u>Alexander Graham Bell</u> invented the telephone.

Who .... ?

5 They found the dinosaur fossil <u>in China</u>.

Where .... ?

many, much, few, little

We use **many** and **few** with countable nouns, and **much** and **little** with uncountable nouns.

In affirmative sentences, we generally use **lots of** or **a lot of** instead of *many* or *much*.

5 **Choose the correct words.**

There were *lots of /* ~~little~~ unusual animals at the zoo.

1 Are there *many / much* birds in this area?

2 There is *few / little* chance of saving this species from extinction.

3 How *much / many* animals are there in the wildlife park?

4 It costs *a lot of / much* money to run a zoo.

5 *Few / Little* people are interested in helping.

6 There are probably *lots of / much* undiscovered species in the Amazon rainforest.

7 *Not much / Few* animal species can survive in the desert.

8 There are *not many / little* rhinos left in the wild.

6 **Complete each second sentence so it means the same as the first sentence. Use *much, many, few* or *little*.**

There is ~~little~~ that can be done about the problem.

1 Not many wild animals live in urban areas.

...... wild animals live in urban areas.

2 There is little natural habitat left here.

There isn't ...... natural habitat left here.

3 Few native tribes still live in the rainforest.

Not ...... native tribes still live in the rainforest.

4 There isn't a lot of money available for wildlife conservation.

There is ...... money available for wildlife conservation.

5 There aren't very many places left where this species can be found.

There are ...... places left where this species can be found.

6 A lot of the original landscape has disappeared.

...... of the original landscape can still be seen.

for example, such as, including, also, too, as well

The linking words/phrases **for example**, **such as** and **including** are used to introduce examples of something.

The linking words **also** and **too** are used to show that something is similar to what was mentioned in the sentence before.

- **For example** is used at the beginning of a new sentence, and is followed by **subject + verb**. *For example* is followed by a comma.

  *Many species may be facing extinction in the wild. **For example**, there are very few pandas or tigers in their natural habitat.*

- **such as** and **including** join the example(s) to the first part of the sentence. We put a comma before *such as*, *like* and *including*.

  *There are many endangered species, **such as/ including** pandas and tigers.*

- **also, too** and **as well** show the similarity between the ideas in two sentences, but they not join them into one sentence.

  *Deforestation destroys wildlife habitats. It can **also** produce greenhouse gases.*

  *Deforestation destroys wildlife habitats. It can produce greenhouse gases **too/as well**.*

7 **Choose the correct words.**

There are several different categories of musical instruments.

For example / ~~Including~~*, there are all sorts of stringed instruments, [1] also / including the guitar, the violin, the cello and so on. The harp is a stringed instrument [2] also / as well. There are [3] also / too wind instruments, [4] such as / for example the flute and the clarinet. Another category is percussion instruments, which include the various types of drums and the xylophone [5] for example / too.*

8 **Complete the text with *for example, such as, including, also, too* or *as well*. In some gaps there is more than one possible answer, but use each word/phrase once only.**

London's best-known landmark is probably the clock tower of Big Ben, but the city has other famous landmarks [1] .... [2] ...... , there is Tower Bridge, which lifts up in the middle to let ships pass underneath. London has [3] ...... got several famous churches, [4] ...... Westminster Abbey, where the kings and queens are crowned, and St Paul's Cathedral. A two-hour tour on a double-decker bus will take you past these and dozens of other famous historical buildings, [5] ...... Buckingham Palace and the Tower of London. Not all of London's landmarks are historical, though – there are modern landmarks [6] .... One example of these is the London Eye, which looks like a giant bicycle wheel.

Review Units 3 and 4

Grammar: present perfect and past simple

1 Circle the correct option.

1 I *went / have been* to the cinema last week.
2 We *did / have done* an exam yesterday.
3 It *has snowed / snowed* three times this week.
4 When *did you / have you* become a vegetarian?
5 A new sports centre *opened / has opened* in our town.
6 Really? When *did it open / has it opened*?
7 William *has gone / went* to rugby practice. He'll be back later.
8 The dodo *became / has become* extinct in 1750.

1 mark per item: ...... / 8 marks

2 Complete the sentences with *ever, never, for* or *since*.

1 I've had a sore throat .... Wednesday.
2 Have you .... been in hospital?
3 Sylvia has .... eaten wild boar.
4 Our family lived in Vienna ....…... three years.
5 I've been a vegetarian .... I was twelve.
6 We've been here ....…. the last three hours.

1 mark per item: ...... / 6 marks

3 Write present perfect sentences with *already, just* and *yet*.

I / go to the gym / today (already)
I've already been to the gym today.

1 I / make / a pizza. (just)

....

2 You / see / the doctor? (yet)

....

3 John / finish / his lunch. (already)

....

4 She / not take / her medicine. (yet)

....

5 Sarah / go to bed. (just)

....

2 marks per item: ...... / 10 marks

4 Complete the sentences with the correct form of the verbs in brackets (present perfect or past simple).

1 My family ....….... (have) flu last Christmas.
2 I ....…... (break) my leg in February.
3 Kirsty ....….. (be) ill this week.
4 We ....….. (not see) any foxes in our garden this year.
5 Pete ....…..... (work) as a zookeeper since 2008.

1 mark per item: ...... / 5 marks

Present simple and past simple passive

5 Complete the sentences with the correct form of the verbs in brackets (present or past passive).

1 Tsunamis ....…... (cause) by earthquakes.
2 Our house ....…... (build) in 1998.
3 We ....….. (rescue) from the flood by helicopter.
4 Brown bears ....…... (find) in North America.
5 Many people ....…... (hurt) in the accident.

1 mark per item: ...... / 5 marks

6 Complete the text with the correct form of the verbs in brackets (present or past passive).

Nowadays many wild animals [1] ....…... (hunt) in Europe, including rabbit and wild boar. Rabbit and boar are both popular dishes in countries such as France, Italy and Spain, where they [2] ....…... (eat) in restaurants and at home. In the past, bison [3] ....…... (kill) for their meat. However, today they [4] ....…... (protect) and can only be found in Poland. Deer meat has been popular for a long time. It [5] ....…... (serve) regularly at royal feasts during the 18th century.

2 marks per item: ...... / 10 marks

Few, little, much, many, lots

7 Complete the second sentence so that it has the same meaning as the first sentence. Use *few, little, much, many* and *lots*.

1 Many people don't like snakes.

...................…. of people don't like snakes.

2 They gave us little information about the animals.

They didn't give us ....…. information about the animals.

3 There were a lot of insects inside the tent.

There were ....….. insects inside the tent.

4 Most of the food was eaten at the party.

Not ....…. food was left after the party.

5 Not many rats survived the Great Fire of London.

...................…. rats survived the Great Fire of London.

6 We had so much to do that there wasn't much time for talking.

We were so busy that there was ....…. time for talking.

1 mark per item: ...... / 6 marks

Vocabulary: health and illness

8 Circle the correct option.

1 A: I've got a *rash / sore throat* on my face.

  B: Why don't you use some of this *skin cream / cough medicine*?

2 A: I've got a high *temperature / headache* and I ache a lot.

  B: You should take two *painkillers / eardrops* and go to bed.

3 A: Do you have a *healthy / fit* lifestyle?

  B: Yes, I do. And I never take *junk food / drugs*.

1 mark per item: ...... / 6 marks

The environment

9 Complete the sentences with words about the environment.

1 The a................. in the Alps killed two skiers.

2 When was the last volcanic e.................... ?

3 T............ can carry animals across many miles.

4 The biggest waves in the world are t..............

5 After six months of no rain, there was a terrible d......................

6 Many natural h.............. are being destroyed.

7 P............ from industry goes into seas and rivers.

1 mark per item: ...... / 7 marks

Wild animals

10 Circle the odd one out.

1 *Owls / Goats / Bats* hunt at night.

2 *Lynx / Tigers / Wolves* are large cats.

3 *Beavers / Otters / Storks* have sharp teeth and live in rivers.

4 *Boar / Deer / Owls* are sometimes killed for their meat.

5 *Eagles / Bats / Storks* build nests at the top of tall trees.

6 *Rabbits / Bears / Deer* are timid animals that eat grass.

1 mark per item: ...... / 6 marks

False friends

11 Label the pictures.

1 ....

2 ....

3 ....

4 ....

1 mark per item: ...... /4 marks

12 Complete the sentences.

1 My brother lives in a small a.................... in the city centre.

2 The police couldn't find any e.................... at the crime scene.

3 Smoking is a very bad h......................

4 The a.................... went well and I got a part in the play.

5 We need to turn round. We're going in the wrong d.....................

6 On our trip to China, we saw some spectacular mountain s.....................

7 I have just finished reading a brilliant n..................... by Lois Duncan.

8 My sister never agrees with me. We have lots of a.....................

1 mark per item: ...... / 8 marks

Adjective + preposition

13 Complete the sentences with a word from each box.

~~afraid~~ ashamed better confused fed up interested nervous worried	about about at by in of of with

Are you *afraid of* spiders?

1 I always get very .... going on stage – even though I really love performing!

2 I'm .... doing the same thing every day!

3 She isn't very .... cooking.

4 We were .... the instructions in the exam.

5 Neil is .... sports than languages.

6 My dog is ill and I'm .... her.

7 Owen is .... his bad behaviour.

2 marks per item: ...... / 14 marks

Linking words

14 Complete the text with the linking words in the box.

also   although   however   including   too

We have good weather most of the time here and in summer it's very hot and sunny. [1] ...., in August and September we are often hit by big storms. Recently, we have experienced a lot of floods, [2] ....
In 2006, a violent storm destroyed many buildings, [3] .... the school and the local sports stadium. The storm [4] .... damaged many people's homes. [5] .... nobody was killed, a few people were injured. A year later, the whole town was flooded.

1 mark per item: ...... / 5 marks

Total marks: ...... / 100

5A Me and my family

Vocabulary: appearance

1 Complete the mind map with the words in the box.

| dreadlocks | dyed | earrings | make-up | nail varnish |
| necklace | ring | shaved head | spiky | stud | tattoo |

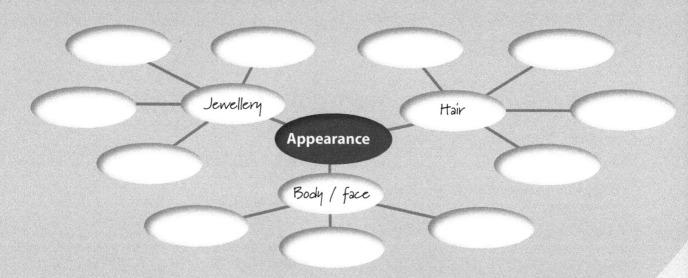

2 Add the words in the box to the diagram in Exercise 1.

| bracelet | curly | dark | fair |
| scar | straight | watch |

3 Complete the sentences with words from Exercise 1.

1 When a couple gets married, they usually give each other a ....

2 Famous women who have had a .... include Britney Spears, Demi Moore and Sinead O'Connor. They soon grew their hair back again!

3 Now I've got pierced ears, I spend all my money on ....

4 Reggae singers often have ....

5 Punk rockers are well-known for their amazing, ... hairstyles.

6 Goths often have .... black hair.

7 You can buy .... in many different colours. Most women prefer red or pink, but blue and black are also fashionable!

8 Most people who have a pierced nose wear a small .... They don't usually wear a ring in their noses.

Working with words: compound adjectives

4 Complete the sentences with a compound adjective.

1 I'm a bit afraid of my uncle Bill and I never talk to him. He's too ....-........... .

2 Mr Jones must spend a lot of money on clothes: he is always very ....-........... .

3 Caroline usually wears ....-........... shoes for work.

4 He thinks he's really ....-........... !

5 The Green family live in a ....-........... building.

6 We have ....-........... heating in our house.

5 Circle the correct option.

1 My parents aren't very *open-minded* / *self-confident*. They won't let me have pierced ears.

2 Children can be very *confident* / *self-centred*. They have to learn to share.

3 My sister has just had a beautiful, *blue-eyed* / *blue-haired* baby.

4 My mum doesn't get angry if I forget to tidy my room. She's very *open-minded* / *easy-going*.

5 Our cousin is really *old-fashioned* / *well-dressed*. He hasn't got a mobile phone or a computer and he always wears a tie, even at the weekend.

6 Most Japanese people are naturally *straight-haired* / *blond-haired*.

6 Complete the sentences with the words in the box.

each other	herself	myself	ourselves
themselves	yourselves		

1 Do you like my necklace. I made it ....

2 My two-year-old sister took my scissors out of my pencil case and cut ....

3 My little brothers always help .... to get dressed in the mornings.

4 There's food and drink for everybody on the table. Just help ....!

5 We went skating yesterday. Harriet and Joanna fell over and hurt .... on the ice.

6 My parents let us decorate our bedrooms .... My sister painted hers black!

Grammar: permission and obligation

7 Circle the option that isn't possible.

Susan *can* / *is allowed to* / *must* buy anything she wants.

1 Daniel *can't* / *mustn't* / *isn't allowed* go into his brother's room.

2 Our teacher *allowed us to* / *let us* / *have us* go home early last Friday.

3 *Can you* / *Have you* / *Are you allowed to* stay out late at night?

4 In the seventies, girls *must* / *had to* / *were made to* wear a skirt to school.

5 Tomorrow is the last day to enter the competition, so I *can* / *must* / *have to* finish this painting tonight!

6 The coach was angry with the team. *He made them* / *They couldn't* / *They had to* run round the pitch ten times!

8 Complete the second sentence so it means the same as the first sentence. Use the correct form of the word in brackets.

1 I can ride my cousin's motorbike. (let)
My cousin .... his motorbike.

2 I can't have a TV in my bedroom. (allow)
I'm .... have a TV in my bedroom.

3 We must take our shoes off before we go into the house. (make)
My mum .... take off our shoes before we go into the house.

4 It is my job is to wash the car every Saturday morning. (have to)
I .... the car every Saturday morning.

5 Does your mum let you stay out after ten o'clock? (allow)
Are .... stay out after ten o'clock?

9 Complete the text with the words in the box.

are allowed	can	don't have to	lets
makes	not allowed to		

My aunt and uncle live in Iráklia, which is a small, Greek island in the Mediterranean. They run a small hotel and I usually stay with them during the summer – and it's great! My cousin and I ¹ .... to do what we want most of the time. We ² .... swim in the pool, play table tennis or go to the beach. Sometimes, when it's really busy, we help in the hotel restaurant. We ³ .... help, but it's actually good fun. I enjoy making the coffees behind the bar. On Mondays, my aunt doesn't work and we go out fishing on her boat. I'm ⁴ .... sail on my own though. On Tuesdays, my uncle goes to the market and buys fresh fruit and vegetables for the restaurant. He usually ⁵ .... us go with him, to help carry all the things back to the car. The market also has a lot of stalls that sell jewellery and clothes. After we have done the shopping, my uncle ⁶ .... us look around the stalls while he goes to the bank or the post office. Every week, I buy a new pair of earrings or a necklace!

Reading

1 **Look at the photos. Tick (✓) the things you can see.**

costumes ☐ dyed hair ☐ tattoo ☐
piercing ☐ earrings ☐ nose-stud ☐
stud ☐ make-up ☐

a

b

2 **Write the correct title (a or b) for each text in the space provided.**

a Body art **b** Body jewellery

3 **Read the article again and match the paragraphs (1–6) with the headings (a–f).**

a Symbols of strength

b A fashion which broke the law

c An ancient art

d A new royal fashion

e A fashion for everyone

f The latest trend for young people

4 **Read the article again. Are the sentences true or false?**

	T	F
1 The oldest tattooed mummy was found in ancient Egypt.	☐	☐
2 Natives in the Pacific gave English sailors their first tattoos.	☐	☐
3 In the 1700s, members of the royal court were not allowed to have tattoos.	☐	☐
4 Body piercing has always been most popular amongst poor people.	☐	☐
5 In the sixteenth century, nobody was allowed to have pierced. noses or nipples	☐	☐
6 In the seventeenth century, men couldn't wear earrings.	☐	☐

1 ....
What do Egyptian mummies and Hollywood celebrities have in common? The answer is tattoos. Stars like Angelina Jolie and Johnny Depp are famous for their tattoos. You may think this is a new fashion, but tattoos have existed since Neolithic times. In 1991, the mummified body of a man who lived 53 centuries ago was found in the Alps. Ötzi the Iceman had 57 tattoos on his back and legs. Tattoos have also been discovered on mummies from ancient Egypt and Russia, but Ötzi is even older. The fact is that the most ancient human skin ever discovered is tattooed.

2 ....
The English explorer, Captain James Cook, was responsible for bringing the fashion for tattoos to Europe. During the 1700s, he visited the Pacific islands where he and his men were amazed by the tattoos they saw on the bodies of the natives. Many sailors returned to England with tattoos and the royal court was fascinated. King George V returned from China with a tattoo of a dragon on his arm. Other European kings also had tattoos, and the fashion for tattoos became popular with rich people.

3 ....
Nowadays, tattoos are worn by many different people, from the rich and famous to teenagers and even granddads!

4 ....
Walk through any city centre on a busy Saturday, and you can see teenagers with rings through their noses and lips – and with studs in their tongues. In the summer, both boys and girls wear short T-shirts to show the piercings on their stomachs.

5 ....
However, body piercing is nothing new. Like tattoos, body piercing was popular with ancient cultures, such as the Egyptians and the Romans. Roman centurions, including Julius Caesar, had body piercing as a symbol of their strength. Nose rings and pierced lips were also common among tribes on the American continent, both as symbols of strength and for religious reasons.

6 ....
Explorers who travelled to the America introduced body piercing to Europeans The fashion spread quickly and has bee popular ever since. In the sixteenth century, almost everyone who was rich had pierced ears or noses. The only tim when piercing was not in fashion was during the seventeenth century when the church introduced strict rules. Body piercing was against the law and only women were allowed to wear earrings.

Grammar: relative pronouns and relative clauses

5 **Join the sentences in columns A and C with a relative pronoun in column B. Sometimes more than one answer is possible.**

	A	B	C
1	The Arctic is the only place		people like to relax.
2	Twins are brothers or sisters	which	my sister was born.
3	Beijing is the city	who	means 'to be friends again'.
4	2002 was the year	that	wears a nose-stud
5	There's a girl in my class	where	were born at the same time.
6	*Make up* is a phrasal verb	when	you can see wild polar bears.
7	The weekends are		the 2008 Olympics were held.

6 **Complete the sentences with *when*, *where*, *which* or *who*.**

George V was the king of England *who* had a dragon tattoo on his arm.

1 Identical twins are two people born at the same time .... look exactly alike.

2 The Webcafé is an internet café .... there are a lot of computers.

3 The 1930s was a terrible time .... many people were very poor.

4 Tattoos are a fashion .... started centuries ago.

5 China is a country .... families can only have one child.

6 Look! There's Mike with a girl. Can you see .... she is?

7 **Read the sentences in Exercise 6 again. In which sentence(s) can you use *that*?**

Listening

8 🔘 **5.1** **Listen to Beth and Jenny talking about being identical twins. Write their names under the pictures.**

....

....

9 **Listen again and answer the questions.**

1 Which twin says that she and her sister are best friends?

2 How often do the twins argue?

3 Which twin makes up first after an argument?

4 What trick did they play when they were younger?

5 Who has a boyfriend?

6 What do the girls say is more difficult when you are a twin?

Working with words: phrasal verbs for relationships

10 **Circle the correct option.**

1 I *went out with / fell out with* my best friend yesterday and we're not speaking to each other.

2 Andrea *takes after / looks after* her grandmother. They are both very competitive.

3 Everyone in the team *looks up to / makes up with* Mr Trainer. He's a really brilliant coach!

4 Tanya is *getting on with / going out with* a boy from the swimming club.

5 Mark and Joanne had a terrible argument last week, but they finally *made up / broke up* yesterday and are together again.

6 Chris *looks after / breaks up with* his cousins every Friday night while his aunt and uncle go out.

Useful expressions

1 Complete the expressions with the words in the box.

| about bad believe down end say up ~~wrong~~ |

What's ......*wrong*......?

1 Cheer .... !
2 Go on! What did he .... ?
3 I can't .... that!
4 That's not so ....
5 Calm ....
6 Tell me all .... it.
7 It's not the .... of the world.

2 Complete the dialogues. Choose the correct option (a or b).

Tanya: Hi, Katie. Did you have a good weekend?
Katie: No, I didn't. And now I'm really upset.
Tanya: Why? ¹ ....
Katie: My parents have bought a house in Redtown. I'm leaving the school next month.
Tanya: Well. ² .... Redtown isn't very far away. We can still see each other at the weekends.
Katie: Yes, I know. But I don't know anybody in Redtown.
Tanya: ³ .... I'm sure you can make new friends there.
Katie: Yes. But I don't want to go! I like it here!

1 **a** Cheer up! **b** What's wrong?
2 **a** It's not the end of the world.
　　b Go on! What did they say?
3 **a** Cheer up! **b** What happened?

Mum: Hello Luke. Did you have a good day at school?
Luke: No. It was awful!
Mum: Why? What happened?
Luke: Mr Painter didn't like my art project.
Mum: ⁴ .... Your project was brilliant!
Luke: Well, Mr Painter didn't think so.
Mum: Why not? Did he say he didn't like it?
Luke: Not exactly. He ...
Mum: ⁵ .... What did he say?
Luke: He said that Mark's project is better than mine.
Mum: ⁶ .... You can't always be the best.

Luke: Yeah. I know. But I worked really hard on that project.
Mum: I know you did. ⁷ .... I'm sure you can do better than Mark next time.

4 **a** What's wrong? **b** I can't believe that!
5 **a** Go on! **b** It's not the end of the world.
6 **a** That's not so bad. **b** Go on!
7 **a** Cheer up! **b** Tell me all about it.

3 Complete the dialogue with the sentences (a–g) below. There is one extra sentence.

Tina: Hi. Amy. Can I come in?
Amy: Yeah. Sure.
Tina: Amy? Are you OK?
Amy: No, I'm not. I feel terrible!
Tina: ¹ ....
Amy: It's Ian! I hate him!
Tina: ² ....
Amy: Thanks.
Tina: ³ ....
Amy: I saw him with another girl. They were sitting together in the park.
Tina: ⁴ ....
Amy: But they were sitting very close! I think they were holding hands!
Tina: ⁵ ....
Amy: Exactly! I think he's going to break up with me!
Tina: ⁶ ....
Amy: Really? How do you know?
Tina: It's obvious! He is always phoning you up.

a Calm down. Here, have a drink of water.
b That's not so bad. Maybe she's a friend from drama club.
c Well, it's not the end of the world. I know that Danny likes you.
d Why? What's wrong?
e Cheer up! Let's go out and have some fun!
f OK. Now tell me all about it.
g I can't believe that! He's going out with you!

Pronunciation: homonyms

4 🔊 **5.2** **Listen to six sentences which form a dialogue. Circle the correct option for each sentence.**

leave(/live)

1 no / know **4** there / their
2 bare / bear **5** there / they're
3 wear / where **6** hear / here

Writing: a description of a person

5 **Read Luke's description of his grandmother. Which question did he answer (a, b or c)?**

a Who do you take after the most in your family?

b Who is the most important person in your family?

c Who do you get on with best at home?

6 **Read the description again and match the headings (a–d) with the paragraphs (1–3). There is one extra heading.**

a A love of sport
b What we look like
c Our friends
d Our other interests

7 **Complete the description with *both* or *neither*.**

8 **Complete the sentences. Choose the correct option (a, b or c).**

1 Luke and his grandmother are .... athletic.
   a neither   **b** both   **c** both of

2 Luke's grandmother likes cycling and .... does Luke.
   a neither   **b** both   **c** so

3 .... them are competitive.
   a Both of   **b** Both   **c** Neither

4 .... them spends a lot of time at home.
   a Both of   **b** Neither of   **c** So

5 Luke isn't shy, and .... is his grandmother.
   a so   **b** neither   **c** both

6 They .... meeting new people.
   a like both   **b** both like **c** neither like

7 They .... very talkative.
   a so are   **b** both are   **c** are both

1

I am very similar to my mother's side of the family, especially my grandmother. We ¹ .... have thick, wavy hair and blue eyes. ² .... of us are fair-skinned and in summer we get sunburned easily. We're ³ .... tall, slim and athletic. My grandmother is the same weight as she was in her thirties!

2

We ⁴ .... love sport. When she was younger, my grandmother was a brilliant cyclist. She still goes cycling at the weekends with her friends, even though she's nearly seventy! Like most sporty people, my grandmother is very competitive – and so am I! We ⁵ .... like winning. Sometimes we go cycling together along country roads. ⁶ .... of us likes to be behind the other one. We ⁷ .... like to be in front! Sometimes I let her go in front because she shouldn't cycle too fast at her age!

3

When we are not competing we get on really well. We're ⁸ .... artistic and enjoy going to art exhibitions. We're also ⁹ .... out-going and friendly. ¹⁰ .... of us is shy. My grandmother lives alone but she goes out a lot with her friends – and so do I! ¹¹ .... of us spends a lot of time at home watching TV. We're self-confident and love going out and meeting new people. We can talk to anyone. In fact, my dad says we ¹² .... talk too much, which is probably true!

9 **Choose a friend who you get on really well with and make notes. Say how you get on, how you are similar and how you are different. Then write a description.**

10 **Check your writing.**

Have you used *both* and *neither* correctly?

Have you written two or three clear paragraphs?

Have you checked your spelling and punctuation?

Reading

1 **Read the text and choose the correct option (a, b or c).**

Dear Gran,

I hope you are ¹ .... I'm sending you a photo of me and my girlfriend, Alanna. She's very friendly and cheerful. We ² .... on really well all the time! Alanna likes sport, too, and we do ³ .... of things together. Last week, we ⁴ .... ice skating. Why don't we all go cycling together one weekend?

Love,

Luke

1 a good   **b** best   **c** well

2 a go   **b** make   **c** get

3 a lots   **b** many   **c** much

4 a went   **b** have been   **c** were going

2 **Read the text and choose the correct option (a, b or c).**

Hi Katie,

How are you? What's your new school like? Have you ¹ .... any new friends, yet? I miss you a lot. There's a new girl in our class ² .... comes from Australia. She's really attractive and ³ .... and she's already got a boyfriend! She's ⁴ .... with Luke Thomson!

See you soon,
Tanya

1 a done   **b** taken   **c** made

2 a she   **b** who   **c** which

3 a pleased   **b** self-confident   **c** self-centred

4 a going out   **b** falling out   **c** getting on

Listening

2 🎧 **5.3** **Listen to the message. What times does the shop close on Saturday?**

3 🎧 **5.4** **Listen to the conversation. Which person is she talking about?**

Word list Unit 5

ancestor (n)	....	embarrassing (adj)	....	respect (n)	....
annoying (adj)	....	embryo (n)	....	select (v)	....
argue with somebody	....	emperor (n)	....	self-centred (adj)	....
attention (n)	....	extinction (n)	....	shaved head (n)	....
bad-tempered (adj)	....	fall out (phr v)	....	socialise (v)	....
be allowed to (phr)	....	go out (with somebody) (phr v)	....	society (n)	....
be annoyed with somebody (phr)	....	government (n)	....	spiky hair (n)	....
break up with somebody (phr)	....	high-heeled shoes (n)	....	stud (n)	....
bride (n)	....	independent (adj)	....	tongue (n)	....
broadband (adj)	....	knock (n)	....	touch (v)	....
cell (n)	....	lamb (n)	....	twin (n)	....
cheer somebody up (phr)	....	lips (n pl)	....	unbelievable (adj)	....
clever (adj)	....	lonely (adj)	....	under pressure (adj phr)	....
community (n)	....	make up (with somebody) (phr v)	....	upset (adj)	....
confused (adj)	....	marriage (n)	....	**U5 Reading Explorer**	
connection (n)	....	nail varnish (n)	....	adolescence (n)	....
couple (n)	....	necklace (n)	....	apron (n)	....
custom (n)	....	obey (v)	....	baptise (v)	....
do well (v phr)	....	obligation (n)	....	buggy (n)	....
dragon (n)	....	obvious (adj)	....	chop (v)	....
dreadlocks (n)	....	old-fashioned (adj)	....	community (n)	....
dyed (hair) (adj)	....	open-minded (adj)	....	firewood (n)	....
easy-going (adj)	....	permission (n)	....	hidden (adj)	....
		pierced ears (n)	....	mix with (v)	....
		preserve (v)	....	rebellious (adj)	....
				relaxed (adj)	....

Grammar Practice Unit 5

permission and obligation

- **Permission** is about things we want to do; laws, rules, parents, etc. tell us which things we *can* do and which things we *can't* do.

  Can has the same form for all subjects and is followed by the **bare infinitive**. The negative is *can't (cannot)* and it is the same for all subjects. The past form is *could*.

  *We **can/can't** wear jeans at school.*

  If you *let* someone do something, you give them permission to do it. The affirmative is *let/lets* + object + bare infinitive.

  *The school **lets/doesn't let** us wear jeans.*

- *Let* cannot used in the passive.

  Allow has the same meaning as *let*, but the affirmative is *allow/allows* + object + full infinitive.

  *The school **allows/doesn't allow** us to wear jeans.*

- *Allow* can be used in the passive; it is followed by the **full infinitive**.

*We **are/aren't allowed to** wear jeans at school.*

- Obligation is usually about things we don't want to do; laws, rules, parents, etc. tell us which things we *must* do, and which things we *mustn't* do, even by mistake.

  Must has the same form for all subjects and is followed by the **bare infinitive**. The negative is *mustn't*. The past form is *had to*.

  *Students **must** be quiet in class. They **mustn't** talk during a test.*

  We use *have to* about what is necessary – because of a rule/law/etc, or because of the situation. We form the affirmative with *have/has to* + bare infinitive. We form the negative and questions in the same way as with normal verbs. The past form is *had to*.

  *We **have to** wear a school uniform.   **Do I have to** eat all this food?*

  If you *make* someone do something, you give them an order and so they do it. The affirmative is *make/makes* + object + bare infinitive.

*Our teachers **(don't) make** us do a lot of homework.*

1 **Choose the correct words.**

You *mustn't / ~~aren't allowed~~* make a lot of noise.

1 Her parents never *let / allow* her to stay out late.

2 You *mustn't / don't have to* do it, but you can if you like.

3 *Can / Must* I go out tonight, please?

4 We aren't *let / allowed* to go out except at weekends.

5 I *didn't have to / mustn't* finish my project yesterday.

6 Jay's dad *made / was made* him stay at home last night.

7 We *made / were made* to clean up the art room after the lesson.

8 You *don't have to / mustn't* park here – it's not allowed.

2 **Complete the sentences with the correct infinitive form of the verbs in the box.**

answer	be	borrow	~~listen~~
stay	tidy		watch

My sister won't let me *listen* to her new CD.

1 Can I .... a pencil, please?

2 My mum always makes me .... my room.

3 Children under 15 aren't allowed .... this movie.

4 'Mike, you must .... home by nine o'clock.'

5 Matt was made .... behind after school to finish his history essay.

6 'I'm sorry, but I can't .... any questions right now.'

3 **Complete each second sentence so it means the same as the first sentence. Use the words in brackets.**

They don't let us wear jewellery at school. (allowed)

We aren't *allowed to wear jewellery at school.*

1 Liza often has to look after her little sister. (made)

Liza is often ....

2 It isn't necessary to spend hours studying for the test. (have to)

You ....

3 I have to phone my parents if I'm going to be home late. (must)

My parents say I ....

4 We have to wear tracksuits for PE lessons. (make)

They ....

5 Jill isn't allowed to wear a stud in her nose. (let)

Jill's mum ....

6 They won't let me go out until I finish my homework. (can't)

I ....

reflexive pronouns and *each other*

We use **reflexive pronouns** with verbs such as *burn, cut, hurt, kill, look at, teach*, etc. when the same person is both the subject and the object of the verb.

*Sam hurt **himself**.*

We use ***each other*** when person A does something to person B, and person B does the same thing to person A.

She looked at him. He looked at her.
*= They looked at **each other**.*

4 **Complete the sentences with reflexive pronouns or *each other*.**

Jack and Lauren get on well with *each other*.

1 They injured ...... while they were rock climbing.

2 I was nervous before the test, but then I told ...... not to worry.

3 Why are Lee and Aneta shouting at ...... ?

4 She made ...... a really nice bracelet.

5 We went to a football match and we saw ...... on the giant screen.

6 Jack and Lauren always give ...... birthday presents.

7 He was angry with ...... for missing an easy goal.

8 Robbie and Fran send ...... text messages every day.

relative clauses

We use a **relative clause** to give extra information about the main part of a sentence.

We place a **relative pronoun** (*who, which*) or **relative adverb** (*when, where*) after the noun it relates to, followed by the rest of the relative clause.

We use: • ***who*** for people • ***when*** for times
          • ***which*** for things • ***where*** for places

*Summer is **the time when** people go to the beach.*

***The dog which** chases us belongs to our neighbours.*

5 **Complete the sentences with *who*, *which*, *where* or *when*.**

Look! She's the girl *who* sits next to Lauren in class.

1 I loved the place ...... we went on holiday last year.

2 The person ...... annoys me the most is my brother.

3 The time of day ...... I relax is in the evening.

4 One animal ...... is common in this area is the fox.

5 The classroom ...... we have French is at the end of the corridor.

6 **Join the sentences using *who, which, where* or *when*.**

The old man is very bad-tempered. He lives in that house.

The old man who lives in that house is very bad-tempered.

1 One problem is greenhouses gases. It is extremely serious.

....

2 They lived in a time. Changes happened more slowly then.

....

3 The little town is a busy city now. He grew up there.

....

4 The boys have been punished. They broke the window.

....

both and *neither*

We use ***both (of)*** and ***neither (of)*** to show that two things are the same in some way.

We use ***both of*** + **object pronoun** in an affirmative statement.

*Lauren plays tennis. Jack plays tennis. = **Both of** them play tennis.*

We use ***neither of*** + **object pronoun** in a negative statement.

*You **don't** like tennis. I **don't** like tennis. = **Neither of** us likes tennis.*

Both takes a verb in the **plural**; ***neither*** takes a verb in the **singular**.

Both (without *of*) comes before the main verb, but after the verb *be*.

7 **Complete each second sentence so it means the same as the first sentence. Use *both, both of* or *neither of*.**

Tracey loves ballet. So do I.

Both *of us love ballet.*

1 She doesn't like break-dancing. Neither do I.
   Neither ....

2 Tracey is quite tall and slim. So am I.
   We're ....

3 She has ballet lessons. So do I.
   We ....

4 She hopes to become a famous ballerina. So do I.
   Both ....

5 She doesn't want to do anything else. Neither do I.
   Neither ....

6A Back to the future

Vocabulary: technology

1 Complete the quiz with the words in the box.

| DVD   earpiece   e-book reader   ~~flat screen~~   memory stick   microchip |
| mobile   modem   MP3 player   palmtop   upload   webcam |

How high-tech are you?

Q1 What technology do you have in your living room?
a a *flat screen* television
b a(n) .... player

Q2 What extras does your computer have?
a a(n) .... – so that I can hear really clearly when I call my friends on Skype.
b a(n) .... – so that I can see my friends when I call them.

Q3 Which gadgets do you usually have in your school bag?
a a(n) .... phone – everyone has one these days!
b a(n) .... – so that I can listen to music any time I want to.
c a(n) .... – it's the easiest way to save documents that I want to use at school.

Q4 Do any of your family or friends have these gadgets?
a a(n) .... in the car
b a(n) .... to help them plan their timetable
c a(n) .... – so that they can download and carry lots of books around with them.

Q5 Do you know how to do these things?
a Find the .... inside the hard drive of your computer.
b .... your photos from your computer onto a webpage.
c Connect the .... to the phone line and to your computer.

2 Do the quiz. Tick (✔) the options that are true for you and score one point for each tick.

3 Read the solutions to the quiz. Complete the texts with the prepositions in the boxes.

11–13 points

| about   for   from   of   on |

You come [1] .... a techno-friendly family. You obviously love technology, but do you spend too much time on your computer and need to work [2] .... your social skills?

7–10 points

You like technology. You aren't an expert, but you know enough [3] .... technology to use the Internet. Your family enjoys technology too, but they don't buy the latest gadgets immediately. They prefer to wait [4] .... the prices to come down. The gadgets in your house probably consist [5] .... at least one computer and a flat-screen TV.

3–6 points

| about   about   for   for   in   to |

You don't have a lot of gadgets. But don't worry [6] .... it! If you know how to use the computer, then you will be fine. However, technology doesn't last [7] .... very long. Make sure you keep up with the changes.

0–2 points

You need to start learning [8] .... technology now! Maybe your parents don't believe [9] .... computers and high-tech science. Talk [10] .... them about how important it is nowadays. Ask them if they will pay [11] .... a computer course.

Grammar: first conditional

4 Match the beginnings of the sentences (1–7) with the endings (a–g).

1 If robots replace teachers,

2 If scientists find a cure for the common cold,

3 If we don't protect the rainforest,

4 If the price of flat-screen TVs comes down,

5 What will people look like in the future

6 If you buy an electric car,

7 Which subjects will I have to study at university

a you won't pollute the environment.

b will your parents buy one?

c if I want to be an astronaut?

d if we can choose our children's genes?

e many animals will become extinct.

f children will be able to study at home.

g we'll be a lot healthier.

Grammar: predicting

5 Complete the sentences with the correct form of the verbs in brackets. Remember to use the present simple after *if*.

1 Marcus (download) .... the files for you, if you (give) .... him your memory stick.

2 If the files (be) .... very big, Nicky (send) .... them in separate messages!

3 If Chloe (want) .... to make free phone calls, she (need) .... to download Skype.

4 If Tim (not tidy) .... his room today, his mum (not let) .... him play computer games.

5 (George / help) .... me change my settings if I (ask) .... him?

6 If Tony (want) .... a new MP3 player, he (have to) .... buy it himself.

6 Read the predictions. Match them with their meanings (a–c).

a The prediction is 100 percent certain.

b The prediction is not 100 percent certain.

c The prediction depends on a condition.

1 People might travel to the moon on holiday. ....

2 Children will all use laptops in the classroom. ....

3 Robots won't learn to show feelings. ....

4 We may live to be 150 years old. ....

5 If we learn more about the physics of time, travel to other galaxies might be possible. ....

6 Scientists might not find a cure for flu. ....

7 Complete the answers to the questions. Use *think / don't think* + *will / won't* and *might*.

Q: What do you think your parents will buy you for your birthday?

A: I *think they might buy me* a new computer. (it's possible)

1 Q: When do you think that we will discover life on other planets?

A: I .... very soon. (I'm sure)

2 Q: Will there be another *Star Trek* film?

A: I .... if the new TV series is successful. (it's possible)

3 Q: Do you think everyone will travel by jetpack?

A: No. I .... (I'm sure)

4 Q: Do you think people will live in space?

A: I .... live in space, but only for a short time. (it's possible)

5 Q: How many children will people have?

A: I .... many children – probably just one. (I'm sure)

Working with words: verb + preposition

8 Circle the correct preposition option.

1 I agree *with / to* William. I think there is life on Mars.

2 Did Maria apologise *about / for* breaking your MP3 player?

3 What do you think *about / of* my new mobile phone?

4 I want everybody in the class to think carefully *about / in* the answer to this question.

5 Mrs Kane is very strict. She doesn't let the students talk *to / about* each other in class.

6 If you argue *to / with* the coach again, you won't be able to play in the next match.

7 My dad's GPS doesn't work. He often complains *for / about* it.

Vocabulary: science subjects

> astronomy biology biochemistry bio-technology
> botany chemistry ecology genetics geology
> physics psychology ~~zoology~~

1 Complete the sentences with the science subjects in the box.

Zoology is the study of animals.

1 .... is the scientific study of chemical processes in biology.

2 Three science subjects taught in schools are ...., ... and ....

3 If you are interested in rocks and fossils, you might enjoy ....

4 The science which combines nature with technology is ....

5 I think .... is a very important subject. Everyone should learn about protecting the environment.

6 .... looks at how the mind works.

7 .... is the study of genes and DNA.

8 If you want to study ...., you will need a telescope.

9 .... is the study of plants and plant life.

Listening

2 🔘 **6.1** Listen to three students talking about the science degree they want to study at university. Match the students with the subjects. There is one extra subject.

1 David ....
2 Leila ....
3 Alice ....

> biochemistry
> bio-technology
> botany
> genetics

3 Listen again. Are the sentences true or false?

	T	F
1 David thinks that genetics is more important than other science subjects.	☐	☐
2 David thinks that geneticists will make people live longer in the future.	☐	☐
3 He believes that geneticists are more intelligent than other scientists.	☐	☐
4 Leila might get bored if she studies bio-technology.	☐	☐
5 She thinks that genetically modified food is dangerous.	☐	☐
6 If Alice studies biochemistry, she'll spend time in the science laboratory.	☐	☐
7 She'll examine cells and describe what things are made of.	☐	☐

Grammar: *going to* for plans and intentions

4 Put the words in the correct order to make sentences.

1 Alice / degree. / going / science / a / to / is / do
....

2 going / other / are / water / look for / to / scientists / American / on / planets.
....

3 Borneo. / to / explore / botanists / A / is / jungle / of / going / in / the / team
....

4 is / school / Our / going / build / new / a / science laboratory. / to
....

5 Read the situations and complete the sentences with *will, might* or *going to*.

1 I'm not sure that I want to go to university. I can't decide.
'I .... not go to university.'

2 The meteorologist is talking about the weather next week.
'If the cold front from Siberia hits England, there .... be snow and ice.'

3 My parents have sold our house and are buying a bigger one.
'We're .... move to a bigger house soon.'

4 Everyone in your family is an artist. Do you want to be the same?
'Are you .... follow the family tradition?'

5 My brother lives in America and is very happy there.
'I don't think my brother .... come back to live in England.'

6 The company wants to test the new vaccine on humans next year.
'The company .... not test the vaccine on humans this year.'

64

Reading

6 **Read the text and match the photos (a–c) with the paragraphs (1–3).**

7 **Read the text again and put the sentences (a–g) in the correct order to complete the summary.**

☐ **a** Even though they've been able to clone animals since 1997, some of the cloned animals haven't lived for very long.

☐ **b** They also believe that they will be able to clone extinct animals.

☐ **c** If they can clone parts of the human body, will they be able to clone complete human beings in the future?

1 **d** Human clones only exist in science fiction; so far, scientists have only been able to clone plants and animals.

☐ **e** When they improve the technology, scientists think they will be able to clone endangered animals.

☐ **f** Researchers are also working on research into human cells.

Clones

Blade Runner, Jurassic Park, Alien: Resurrection, Star Wars: The Clone Wars, Terminal Justice. These films all have something in common: clones.

1 ....

Clones have become a popular theme in Hollywood films. But what exactly are they? In the world of science fiction, clones are humans or other beings that are identical copies of each other. They are often bad or violent and want to take over the world. In real life, cloning involves copying the DNA of living organisms. Scientists have not successfully cloned a complete human being, but they have produced clones of plants, animals and human embryos.

2 ....

The first animal to be cloned from a single adult cell was Dolly, the sheep, in 1997. The DNA from an adult sheep was copied and scientists created an embryo which grew into a lamb. Dolly lived for six years, which is a short time for an adult sheep. Other animals which have been successfully cloned include mice, a cat, a horse, a water buffalo and, in 2009, a camel. If geneticists can produce perfect DNA, they may be able to save endangered animals from extinction.

3 ....

Scientists also dream of cloning extinct animals. This may sound like something from Jurassic Park, but it is not science fiction. In 2002, geneticists in Australia began cloning a Tasmanian Tiger. They used cells from a preserved tiger which died about 65 years ago. The experiment was stopped because the DNA was damaged. There is also a lot of research into cloning human cells. This is called stem-cell research and consists of growing new cells, organs and limbs to use in medicine. In 2008, five human embryos were created from adult skin cells, which were later destroyed. So, what about the future? Will human clones be science fact, or science fiction?

Useful expressions

1 Match the beginnings of the sentences (1–9) with the endings (a–i).

1 How can
2 I'd like to look at
3 Can you explain
4 Could you show
5 I'll show
6 I'll
7 Shall I find
8 Yes,
9 Thank you

a some cheaper models?
b me something more basic?
c of course.
d very much.
e some MP3 players, please.
f I help you?
g how it works?
h take it!
i you our selection.

2 Complete the dialogue. Use phrases from the first column in Exercise 1 to help you.

Customer: Excuse me?

Assistant: Yes. ¹ .... I help you ?

Customer: ² .... some flat-screen TVs, please.

Assistant: Yes, of course. If you follow me, ³ .... you our selection.

Customer: I like this one!

Assistant: It's our best model. It's got all the latest technology.

Customer: Hmm. I don't think I can afford all that. ⁴ .... me some more basic models?

Assistant: How about this one? The picture quality is excellent.

Customer: I like it. ⁵ .... how it works?

Assistant: It's very easy. You just use the remote control. You switch it on with this button here. You can change the channel with …

Customer: That's great, thank you.

Assistant: No problem.

3 Choose the correct option (a, b or c) for each situation.

1 You are in a shop. The shop assistant asks you if you want any help. What does she say?
   a If you follow me, I'll show you our selection.
   b Could you help?
   c How can I help you?

2 You want to ask the shop assistant to show you some webcams. What do you say?
   a Could you show me some webcams, please?
   b I'd like this one, please.
   c Shall I look at some webcams?

3 You want the shop assistant to show you some less expensive webcams. What do you say?
   a I'll take this one!
   b Can you explain how it works?
   c Could you show me some cheaper models, please?

4 You want the shop assistant to explain how an iPod works. What do you say?
   a Could you show me how it works, please?
   b I'd like to see an iPod, please.
   c Shall I show you how it works?

5 The shop assistant offers to show you some cheaper MP3 players. What does she say?
   a Can you show me some cheaper models?
   b Thank you.
   c Shall I find some cheaper models?

6 The shop assistant is showing you a palmtop. You decide to buy it. What do you say?
   a Thank you very much.
   b Yes, of course!
   c I'll take it!

Pronunciation: connected speech

4 **Say the sentences. Underline the words where the sounds are linked.**

1 You switch it on with this button.
2 Put it in your bag.
3 Can you wake me up early?
4 I'd like to look at this one.
5 Turn it down, please!
6 I'll pick you up from school.

5 **🔘 6.2 Listen and check. Practise saying the linked phrases.**

Writing: giving instructions

6 **David's mum is going to Australia for three weeks. Read her instructions. What are they for?**

a using the dishwasher
b washing clothes
c using the oven

Dear David,
While I'm away helping Aunt Sally with her new baby, I'm sure you'll be fine. I know you and Dad can cook and will do the shopping – but don't forget about everything else! Here are the instructions I promised:
1 Empty the basket of dirty clothes onto the floor .... see what you've got.
2 Check you have put all the socks in pairs .... you don't get lots of odd socks.
3 If you've got more light colours, you'll have to wash them first. If you are washing bright colours, wash them on a low temperature .... the colours do not run.
4 Take the washing out as soon as the machine finishes. .... stop the clothes from smelling bad.
5 If it's a nice day, hang the clothes outside. Hang T-shirts and jeans carefully .... you don't have to iron them.
6 When you bring them in, put them on the radiators .... they can finish drying.
Phone me if you have any urgent problems but don't forget the time difference! Australia is 9 hours ahead. Don't forget to email me every day!
Lots of love,
Mum

7 **Read the instructions again and write *so that* or *in order to* in each space.**

8 **Read David's email to his mum. Put the sentences (a–d) in the correct order. Which machine does he want instructions for?**

Dear Mum
...... **a** Dad says we need to use the • but we don't know how to use it.
...... **b** I hope you're having a nice time with Aunt Sally and the baby.
...... **c** Can you send us some instructions?
...... **d** It's rained all week, so we haven't been able to hang the clothes out to dry.
Lots of love,
David

9 **Match the beginnings of the instructions (1–5) with the endings (a–e) and join them with *so that* or *in order to*.**

1 Close the door and select 60 minutes
2 Wait for the machine to finish
3 Put the wettest clothes in the machine first
4 Read the drying instructions on all the clothes
5 Press the 'on' button

a you can open the door safely.
b start the machine.
c check they can go in the dryer.
d all the clothes will dry completely.
e they have time to get dry.

10 **Complete the email from David's mum. Write the instructions from Exercise 9 in a logical order.**

Hi David,
Having a lovely time but missing you lots. Baby Louise is beautiful and Sally and I are having fun.
Anyway, here are instructions for the dryer:
1 ....
....
2 ....
....
3 ....
....
4 ....
....
5 ....
....

Hope the weather gets better. You need some Australian sunshine!
Lots of love,
Mum
P.S. I'll phone you on Sunday.

Listening

1 🔘 6.3 You will hear three people talk about their plans for the weekend. Match the statements (a–d) with the speakers (1–3). There is one extra statement.

Speaker 1 ....
Speaker 2 ....
Speaker 3 ....

  a If it rains, it won't be a problem. We'll still be able to do lots of things.
  b I love science, so I think it'll be great!
  c If the weather's nice, we can go swimming.
  d I think we'll learn a lot about history.

2 🔘 6.4 You will hear someone talk about their favourite book. What is the book about? Choose the correct option (a, b or c).

  a aliens
  b the future
  c ghosts

Reading

3 Put the sentences in a logical order. Choose the correct option (a, b or c).

Dear John and David,
a Here are the instructions for heating them up.
b Finally, press the 'on' button.
c If you want to eat cooked dinners from the freezer, you'll need to use the microwave.
d First, put the food on a plate and cover it with a lid or plastic film.
e When the microwave stops, check your food is hot in the middle.
f Put the plate inside the microwave and select 3 minutes.
Mum

  a c, d, a, f, b, e
  b a, c, d, f, e, b
  c c, a, d, f, b, e

adolescent (n)	....	look at (phr v)	....	team (n)	....
afford (v)	....	magnifying (adj)	....	tell (somebody) off (phr v)	....
ahead (adv)	....	measure (v)	....		
alien (n)	....	Moon (n)	....	translate (v)	....
attract attention (phr)	....	movie (n)	....	turn up (phr v)	....
		odd (adj)	....	universe (n)	....
bend (v)	....	pick up (phr v)	....	unmanned (adj)	....
brain (n)	....	prediction (n)	....	urgent (adj)	....
branch (n)	....	promise (v)	....	wireless (adj)	....
button (n)	....	protect (v)	....	work on (phr v)	....
clone (v)	....	purpose (n)	....	**U6 Reading Explorer**	
collect data (v phr)	....	put on (phr v)	....	Aerodynamic (adj)	....
condition (n)	....	quality (n)	....	air-conditioning system (n)	....
cruel (adj)	....	radiat or (n)	....		
digital (adj)	....	reach (v)	....	cocklebur (n)	....
dress up (phr v)	....	reflect (v)	....	damp (adj)	....
empty (adj)	....	reject (v)	....	design (n)	....
exactly (adv)	....	remote control (n)	....	effective (adj)	....
examine (v)	....	research (n)	....	friction (n)	....
film (n)	....	rock (n)	....	gecko (n)	....
flat screen (n)	....	series (n)	....	hook (n)	....
focus (v)	....	significant (adj)	....	hypodermic needle (n)	....
fossil (n)	....	smell (v)	....		
freezer (n)	....	sock (n)	....	injection (n)	....
ghost (n)	....	soil (n)	....	jagged edge (n)	....
hope (v)	....	spacecraft (n)	....	microscopic (adj)	....
human being (n)	....	spin dryer (n)	....	nest (n)	....
image (n)	....	starring role (n)	....	scales (n pl)	....
incredible (adj)	....	stem (n)	....	specimen (n)	....
influence (v)	....	store (v)	....	spine (n)	....
investigate (v)	....	straight (adj)	....	stick (v)	....
jetpack (n)	....	sunshine (n)	....	termite (n)	....
lens (n)	....	switch on (phr v)	....	thorn (n)	....
lid (n)	....	take over (from somebody) (phr v)	....	treasure chest (n)	....
limb (n)	....				

first conditional

We use the **first conditional** to talk about future actions or predictions which depend on a *condition*, which is another (usually future) event.

The different possibilities in the condition will cause a different result in the future.

*If it **rains** tomorrow, we'll stay at home.*

*If it **doesn't rain** tomorrow, we'll go to the beach.*

The future form we use most often is **will/won't +
bare infinitive**, but we also use the future form of *can* (**will be able to** + bare infinitive) and *must* (**will have to** + bare infinitive).

*If it's cold tomorrow, we **won't be able to** go swimming.*

*If we **move** to London, we'll **have to** find a new home.*

1 Choose the correct words.

If *there's / there'll be* a good film on TV
we watch / we'll watch it.

1 He *must / He'll* have to get broadband if *he
needs / he'll need* a faster connection.

2 If *we go / we'll go* by train *we arrive / we'll arrive*
on Thursday.

3 Susan *can't / won't* be able to contact us if she
doesn't find / won't find her mobile.

4 If prices *continue / will continue* to go down,
I'm / I'll be able to afford a new laptop.

5 *I'll call / I call* you if *there's / there'll be*
anything else I need.

**2 Complete the first conditional sentences with
the form of the verbs in brackets.**

Meera *will go* (go) to university if she *passes*
(pass) her exams.

1 I think I ...... (buy) this mobile phone if it ......
(not be) very expensive.

2 You ...... (not be able) to open the front door
later if you ...... (not take) your key with you.

3 If Ken ...... (not feel) well tomorrow he ......
(have to) stay in bed.

4 The world's climate ...... (change) if we ......
(not prevent) global warming.

5 If scientists ...... (discover) a way to stop
malaria, it ...... (save) millions of lives.

**3 Write first conditional sentences and questions
with these words.**

I / not be able / go out / if I / not finish / my
homework.

*I won't be able to go out if I don't finish my
homework.*

1 If there / be / a problem with your MP3 player
you / have to / take it back to the shop.

....

2 They / not wait / for me if I / not be / there
on time.

....

3 he / be able / download / these files if you /
explain / what to do?

....

4 If there / be / a change of plans we / let / you
know.

....

5 How / you / turn on / the computer if it / not
be / plugged in?

....

predicting

We can use **will**, **may** and **might** to talk about
predictions about the future.

Will, **may** and **might** have the same form for
all subjects (*I, you, he*, etc.). The main verb after
these modals is in the **bare infinitive**.

One day we'll send astronauts to Jupiter.

*They **may** find signs of life on other planets.*

*Our great-grandchildren **might** even travel to other
galaxies!*

The negative of **will** is **won't** (*will not*) and it is
the same for all subjects. The negative of **may**
and **might** is **may not** and **might not**, and these
are also the same for all subjects.

Will usually suggests we are quite sure about
our prediction; **may** suggests we are not so sure;
might usually suggests we are even less sure.
We often use these modals after *I think, I'm sure,*
etc. and/or with words such as *probably, perhaps,
certainly,* etc.

**4 Complete the answers to the questions, using
the words in brackets.**

Will they find life on Mars? (won't)

I'm sure *they won't find life on Mars.*

1 Will the world be a better place in a hundred
years' time? (may)
The world ....

2 Will computers be more powerful ten years
from now? (certainly)
Computers ....

3 Will you travel to the Moon some day?
(might)
I suppose I ....

4 Will aliens ever attack our planet? (never)

I'm sure that ....

5 Will people live longer in the future? (probably)

I think people ....

going to for plans and intentions

We use **be going to** about the future when we have already decided what to do, and we have made some plans.

This may include informal plans about the near future, or plans about our ambitions for something in the distant future.

*Lauren's **going to** row with the rowing club this afternoon.*

*I'**m going to** go to Cambridge next year. I'**m going to** study biology.*

*The government says it's **going to** increase taxes.*

We form the **affirmative** with **am/are/is + going to** + the bare infinitive of the main verb.

We form the **negative** with **am/are/is + not + going to** + the bare infinitive of the main verb.

We make **questions** by putting **am/are/is** before the subject, and then **going to** + the bare infinitive of the main verb.

In **short answers** we use **am/'m not, are/aren't** or **is/isn't**. We don't use the main verb.

> Be careful with *be going* (present continuous) and *be going to* go.
>
> *I'm going to Lee's house now.* (present continuous)
>
> *I'm going to go to America next year.* (going to)

5 **Match the people (1–5) with their plans/ intentions (a–f).**

Ali is in medical school.

1 Carl is learning French.

2 Sara's buying beachwear.

3 Jack is practising the violin.

4 Andy's looking at road maps.

5 Mary has joined a health club.

a go on a summer holiday

b get fit and lose weight

c become a doctor

d hitch-hike around Europe

e find a job in Paris

f play in a concert

6 **Write about the people in Exercise 5 using *going to*.**

Ali is going to become a doctor.

1 ....

2 ....

3 ....

4 ....

5 ....

7 **Write sentences and questions using *going to* with these words.**

you / go / to university in the UK?

Are you going to go to university in the UK?

1 I think / I / become / a teacher.

....

2 Carlos / not / visit / his family this summer.

....

3 Debbie / live / in the south of France?

....

4 we / go / to New York for two weeks.

....

5 I / not / start / studying until after dinner.

....

6 Aneta / help / Jack put music files on his MP3 player.

....

so that and *in order to*

We use **so that** and **in order to** at the beginning of clauses of purpose. This is a part of a sentence which explains why somebody does/did something.

> We form clauses of purpose with:
>
> • *so that* + subject + *can/could* + bare infinitive
>
> • *in order* to + bare infinitive
>
> *I must practise my Spanish **so that** I can talk to people on holiday.*
>
> *My dad goes for long walks **in order to** keep fit.*

8 **Complete the sentences with so *that* or *in order to*.**

He's studying hard *in order to* pass his exams.

1 I'll give you my mobile number ...... you can call me.

2 You have to pay a membership fee ...... join the health club.

3 He got a broadband connection ...... download large files.

4 She took lots of photos on holiday ...... she could show her friends what the place was like.

5 I want a laptop ...... I can work in the school library.

Review Units 5 and 6

Grammar: prepositions

1 Complete the sentences with prepositions. Write – if there is no preposition.

1 I like listening .... soul music.
2 Let's talk .... the holiday.
3 I waited .... you for nearly an hour.
4 Put your hat .... It's freezing outside.
5 Look .... that girl's hair. It's blue and orange!
6 Magda comes .... Portugal.
7 Le Guin's books have been translated .... many languages.
8 Get .... the train quickly! It's leaving!
9 There are two science labs .... our school.
10 Do you believe .... UFOs?
11 I'll phone .... you tomorrow.
12 We're going skating .... next Sunday.
13 My parents don't let me go out late .... night.
14 Are you playing hockey .... the weekend?
15 Do you want to go to the cinema .... Saturday night?

1 mark per item: ..... / 15 marks

2 Complete the phrasal verbs with a preposition.

1 Calm ....! We're not late.
2 It was hot, so she took .... her jacket.
3 My granddad gave .... smoking last year.
4 She thinks her big brother is fantastic. She really looks .... to him.
5 Olivia fell .... her bike yesterday.

1 mark per item: ..... / 5 marks

Permission and obligation

3 Write sentences and questions.

1 We / not / allow / wear make-up / at school.
....
2 your mum / usually / let / you / stay out / late?
....
3 You / must not / run / in the corridor.
....
4 The teacher / make / us / do / extra homework / yesterday.
....
5 My brother / have to / wash the car / every weekend.
....

1 mark per item: ..... / 5 marks

Relative pronouns

4 Write definitions with the relative pronouns *when, where, which* or *who*.

1 A canteen / a place / you / eat lunch.
....
2 A dentist / a person / looks after teeth.
....
3 *Minority Report* / a film / is set in the future.
....
4 Christmas / a time / people / give presents.
....
5 Androids / robots / look like humans.
....

1 mark per item: ..... / 5 marks

5 Complete the sentences with the words in the box.

| his | themselves | himself | itself | each other |

1 Are Mike and Jenny going out with ....?
2 The cat hurt .... when it fell out of the tree.
3 My parents enjoyed .... at the party.
4 My brother cut .... finger with a knife.
5 The baby can't walk by .... yet.

1 mark per item: ..... / 5 marks

Predictions

6 Make first conditional sentences.

1 If I .... (go) shopping tomorrow, ... (you / come) with me?
2 If you .... (break) anything in the shop, you .... (have to) to pay for it.
3 The coach .... (be) angry if John .... (be) late for training again.
4 Mark .... (can) print your photos if you .... (send) him your files.
5 If we .... (not leave) now, we .... (miss) the bus.

2 marks per item: ..... / 10 marks

7 Circle the correct option.

1 I don't think robots *will / might* replace teachers.
2 Ian has got a place at university. He *is going to / will* study engineering.
3 Liz worked very hard so I'm sure she *will / might* pass her exams.
4 The queen *is going to / might* open the new museum next week.
5 I'm sure he *will / won't* come with you. He hates loud music!

1 mark per item: ...... / 5 marks

Vocabulary: phrasal verbs

8 Circle the correct phrasal verb.

1 Don't forget to *pick up / find out* the children from school!
2 I can't believe that Ian and Liz have *broken up / made up*! They were perfect together.
3 You can borrow my new bike, but you must *take after / look after* it!
4 I don't *get on with / fall out with* my twin sister. We always argue.
5 I *take after / look up to* my dad. We look the same and we talk the same!
6 Rosie is *setting off / going out with* a French boy!
7 What did you *find out / look up to* about endangered species?
8 She's always *complaining about / apologising for* the cold, so I've bought her a hat and scarf!

1 mark per item: ..... / 8 marks

9 Circle the odd one out.

1 dreadlocks   dyed   spiky   scar
2 tattoo   earrings   necklace   ring
3 nail varnish   make-up   tattoo   gadget
4 stud   fair   straight   dark
5 upload   webcam   earpiece   modem
6 zoology   physics   biology   botany
7 genetics   biochemistry   ecology   geography

1 mark per item: ..... / 7 marks

Linking words

10 Complete the second sentence so that it means the same as the first. Include *both*, *neither*, *in order to* or *so that*.

1 John hates swimming and Edward hates swimming too.
   They .... swimming.
2 John is friendly and Edward is friendly too.
   They .... friendly.
3 John hates hip-hop and Edward hates hip-hop.
   .... them likes hip-hop.
4 John has fair hair and Edward has red hair.
   .... has dark hair.
5 John is studying medicine because he wants to become a doctor.
   John is studying medicine .... become a doctor.
6 Edward bought a new motorbike because he wants to be able to drive fast.
   Edward bought a new bike .... he can drive fast.
7 Edward didn't have a holiday this summer and John didn't have a holiday either.
   .... them had a holiday this summer.

2 marks per item: ..... / 14 marks

Personality adjectives

11 Circle the correct adjective.

1 When you have a twin you never feel *lonely / self-centred*.
2 I felt very *embarrassed / cheerful* when I fell over in the street!
3 My parents were *disappointed / pleased* when I failed my exams.
4 I was very *anxious / upset* when my boyfriend broke up with me. I cried for three days!
5 She's very *confident / open-minded* and never gets nervous before a performance.
6 Holly is *easy-going / confident*. She's happy to whatever we want to do.
7 He's got big blue eyes and curly, fair hair – he's really *good-looking / well-dressed*.

1 mark per item: ..... / 7 marks

Offering, accepting and refusing help

12 Put the sentences in the dialogue in the correct order.

..... L: Not me. I have to ask my brother to do it and he's fed up with me asking.
..... J: That's not so bad. You can always download them again.
..... J: I can't believe that! Everybody can download MP3 files.
..... J: Cheer up! I'll help you download some music. But first you need to buy a new MP3 player.
..... J: Hi Leila. What's the matter?
..... J: It's not the end of the world.
..... L: I've lost my MP3 player.
..... L: Yes it is. It's got my favourite songs on it.
..... L: No, I can't. I don't know how to download MP3 files.

1 mark per item: ..... / 9 marks

13 Complete the dialogue with the sentences in the box.

How much is it?   I'll take it!   How can I help you?
We'd like to look at some MP3 players, please.
If you follow me, I'll show you our selection.

David: Excuse me.
Assistant: Yes. [1] ....
David: [2] ....
Assistant: Yes, of course. [3] ....
David: Thanks very much.
Assistant: These are our latest models.
Leila: This one looks nice. [4] ....
Assistant: It's £49, which is a very good price.
Leila: That's an excellent price. [5] ....

1 mark per item: ..... / 5 marks

Total marks: ..... / 100

7A Gangs

Vocabulary: cities and towns

1 Match the words in box A with the words in box B to make eight compound nouns.

A	art city ice leisure office public sports youth	B	blocks centres (x3) galleries rinks stadiums transport

1 ....

2 ....

3 ....

4 ....

5 ....

6 ....

7 ....

8 ....

2 Complete the sentences with words from Exercise 1.

1 I think there should be more ....
.... .Young people need places where they can meet and chat, or listen to music.

2 Most large cities have ....
where you can watch a football match or athletics competition.

3 There isn't enough ....
in my neighbourhood. There's only one bus an hour to the city centre and we don't have a train station.

4 There aren't any attractive buildings in our city – just lots of tall ....

5 New York is an important city for culture as well as for business: it's full of ....
.... and museums.

6 There aren't any ....
in my town. If you want to go ice skating you have to travel to the nearest big city.

3 Circle the correct option.

1 Have you ever dropped any *litter / traffic* in the street?

2 There's always a lot of *traffic / graffiti* at five o'clock in the afternoon.

3 There aren't usually many girls at our *skate park / shopping centre*. They prefer shopping!

4 Last night someone broke the windows in the youth centre and covered the walls with *graffiti / crime*.

5 There's too much *crime / shopping centres* in our cities today.

6 We don't like living in the *country / city*. It's too quiet and boring.

Vocabulary: crime

4 Read the definitions and complete the word puzzle. Find the hidden word.

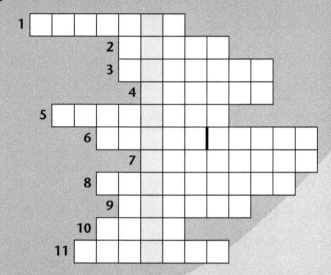

Hidden word: ....

1 A person who sees a crime.

2 A person who steals something.

3 The crime of stealing money from a bank.

4 They wear a uniform and can arrest criminals.

5 A crime that involves somebody entering a house and stealing property.

6 The place where a crime happened.

7 This kind of violence can happen, for example, between fans of the different football teams if they meet after a match.

8 A person who investigates a crime.

9 The person who is affected by a crime.

10 A group of young people who spend time together and are sometimes violent.

11 The crime of attacking a person in the street and stealing their money or their things.

5 Complete the sentences with words in the box.

criminals law robbed stole theft vandalism

1 Do you think graffiti artists are ....?

2 The police have caught the gang that .... the bank.

3 People who break the ....
sometimes go to prison.

4 Graffiti isn't art – it's just ....!

5 Do you know who .... your bike?

6 The biggest news story this week is the
.... of six paintings from the art gallery.

Grammar: reporting verbs

6 Cirlce the correct option to complete the second sentence.

1 'Everybody lie down on the floor!'

The robber *asked / ordered* everybody to lie on the floor.

2 'Nobody move or I'll shoot!'

The robber *warned / reminded* them not to move.

3 'Give me the money!'

The robber *wanted / invited* the bank manager to give him the money.

4 'Put the money in this bag.'

He *warned / told* the bank manager to put the money in the bag.

5 'Can you hold the bag for me, please, while I put the money in it.'

The manager *asked / ordered* the secretary to hold the bag while he put the money in it.

6 'Remember, don't move! Stay right where you are.'

The robber *reminded / wanted* the secretary not to move.

7 Put the words in the correct order to make reported statements.

1 We / to / everyone / invited / come / the / party. / to

....

2 me / The / in / told / for / stay / week. / bed / doctor / a / to

....

3 to / The / us / zoo keeper / touch / animals. / the / warned / not

....

4 asked / My / him / help / brother / me / with / to / homework. / his

....

5 reminded / to / our / lab coats / bring / us / to / The / class. / science teacher

....

6 policemen / the / ordered / gang / stand / to / next to / The / wall. / the

....

Working with words: easily confused words

8 Complete the dialogues with the correct form of the words in the box. There is one extra word.

| borrow   bring   ill   journey   lay   lend   lie   sick |
| take   trip |

A: Can I ¹ .... your *Prison Break* DVDs?

B: Sorry, I've already ² .... them to Mike.

A: We're ³ .... the children to the park on Sunday. Can you come?

B: I'd love to come. Can I ⁴ .... my little cousin, too?

A: Did you enjoy your ⁵ .... to the coast at the weekend?

B: Yes, but the car ⁶..................... was terrible! We had to stop many times because the children felt ⁷ ....

A: I feel really ⁸ .... I've got a headache and a temperature.

B: Why don't you go and ⁹ .... on the sofa for half an hour?

9 Circle the correct options to complete the story.

Last year, I went on holiday to Italy with my two best friends. We had a great time there, but the ¹ *journey / travel* down to the coast was a disaster – our train tickets ² *were stolen / were robbed!* It happened at a station near Rome. It was about five o'clock in the morning, but the station was already very busy. Anyway, we were standing on the platform when a young boy ran past and pushed Tanya to the ground. She ³ *was holding / was keeping* the tickets in her hand, but when she fell, she dropped the tickets on the platform. Another boy, who was standing next to us, quickly picked up the tickets and ran off! We went to the ticket office and ⁴ *told / said* the saleswoman our story. She ⁵ *said / told* that the boys were probably in a gang and ⁶ *told / said* us to call the police – which we did. After that, we bought some more tickets from the saleswoman, who ⁷ *reminded / recalled* us to put them safely in our bags. We then ⁸ *came back / went back* to the empty platform, where we waited for the next train and watched the sun ⁹ *raise / rise*.

Reading

1 Look at the photos. Tick (✓) the things you can see.

a march ☐ parliament ☐ posters ☐
a gun ☐ people ☐ a street ☐ knives ☐

2 Read the article and choose the best heading.

a Violent gangs cause problems on Britain's streets
b Young people fight against gun crime
c The problem of guns in Britain's schools

3 Complete the text with the missing sentences (a–d).

a 'At the beginning, many people said we couldn't change anything.'
b They have also recorded a CD, designed posters and written letters to the government.
c For example, they learn about the law, the media and how to speak in public, as well as how to write letters to politicians.
d The group organised workshops, gave talks to the local community and visited high schools and primary schools.

4 Choose the correct answer (a, b or c).

1 'Youth Act' training sessions usually take place
   a at school.
   b in the evenings.
   c at a neighbour's house.

2 At the training sessions, young people
   a talk about their problems at school.
   b help each other to change their ideas.
   c discuss how to change things in their community.

3 The 'No More Guns' campaign
   a helps young children to learn about the dangers of guns.
   b helps parents to stop using guns.
   c teaches people what to do if they see a gun.

4 Jay says that
   a everyone is more pleased with the CD than the posters.
   b winning the national awards was the best part of the project.
   c the group are proud of the changes they have made.

In Britain, young people aged 11–18 are making changes to their communities. More and more kids are getting involved in 'Youth Act', an organisation that organises citizenship projects in their schools and local communities. They go to after-school training sessions, where they talk about the problems in their neighbourhoods and what they can do to change the situation. This usually involves organising a campaign. At the sessions, they learn all the skills they need to run a successful campaign.[1] .... Very soon, these young people become experts on the problems in their communities.

In some parts of Britain, these problems are very serious. Big cities, such as London and Manchester, have a lot of gun crime and knife crime and young people are often affected. In 2007, a group of young people from Manchester started a campaign against gun crime, called 'No More Guns'. [2] .... 'We want people to know about the problem of gun crime in our neighbourhood', says Joanna, aged sixteen. 'We want to stop gun crime. We believe it's important to teach children about it from a young age. We warn them about the dangers and we teach them what they can do about the problem.'

The 'No More Guns' campaign is one of the most successful youth campaigns in Britain. Its members have been very active. They have worked with the police on an anti-gun project in schools, and have organised two big street marches. [3] .... In 2009, the campaign won three national awards. Jay, one of the boys who wrote the anti-gun song, told us how proud everyone is of the project. 'We are really pleased that the project is working. [4] .... Now, people are more positive. They see that we can make a difference. We've even made the government listen and take action, and gun crime is now a subject that's taught in schools.'

Listening

5 7.1 Listen to an interview with Jessica. What is she talking about?

a a project about using the Internet in schools

b a project about schools in other countries

c a project which involved three different schools working together

6 7.1 Listen again and complete the notes.

Name of project:	^{1}.................... ....
School:	Greencoat School
Partner schools:	in ^{2}.................... and ^{3}....................
Topic chosen:	the ^{4}....................
Result / What we learned	We learnt about African laws and African ^{5}.................... Parents are ^{6}.................... than British parents. The ^{7}.................... is also very important in the community.

Grammar: word order in indirect questions

7 Read the direct questions and then complete the indirect questions from the listening in Exercise 5.

1 What is 'Connecting Classrooms'?
Can you tell me what ....
....?

2 How did you do this?
Could you explain how ....
....?

3 What kind of questions were they?
Can you tell us what kind of questions ....
....?

4 What have you learnt?
Could you tell us something about what ....
....?

8 Write the indirect questions. Use the words in brackets.

What time is it? (can / tell)
Can you tell me what time it is?

1 Who is the president of the football club this year? (know / you)
....

2 What time do the shops open on Saturday morning? (can / tell)
....

3 Where can I buy a newspaper? (could / tell)
....

4 What do we have to do to join the youth club? (anyone / know)
....

5 How do we get to your house from the station? (can / tell)
....

6 Can I borrow a pencil? (could / anyone / lend)
....

Working with words: irregular nouns

9 Complete the sentences with the plural form of the words in the box.

bus	bison	child	country	person	thief

1 You can sometimes see .... in the forests of Poland.

2 How many .... were at the football match yesterday?

3 The famous paintings were stolen from the art gallery by four ....

4 Traditional London .... are painted red.

5 How many different .... competed in the last Olympics?

6 What time do the .... usually go to bed?

10 Circle the correct option.

1 A: I think that *women / woman* are the best cooks.
B: I disagree! Most top chefs are *men / man*.

2 A: Physics *is / are* more interesting than maths.
B: I like science and maths. For me, politics *is / are* the most boring subject.

3 A: Did you see the news on TV last night? *It was / They were* terrible!
B: Yes, I did. I felt very sorry for all those people who *has / have* lost their homes.

Useful expressions

1 **Match the questions (1–4) with the responses (a–d).**

1 Could you give Yasmin a message, please?

2 What's the message?

3 Can you remind her to buy some party decorations?

4 Can you ask her to phone me back?

a Can you tell her to bring some CDs to the party tomorrow?

b Yes, of course. I'll ask her to call you when she gets home.

c Yes, of course.

d OK. I'll tell her.

2 **Complete the dialogue with expressions from Exercise 1.**

Declan: Hello. Can I speak to Yasmin, please?

Mrs Osman: No, sorry. She's not home at the moment. Who's speaking?

Declan: It's Declan, from school. ¹ ....?

Mrs Osman: ² .... What's the message?

Declan: It's about the music for the twins' birthday. ³ ....?

Mrs Osman: Yes, of course.

Declan: And there are some other things I need to ask her as well. ⁴ ....?

Mrs Osman: OK.⁵ .... She will be back about 7 o'clock.

Declan: Thank you very much, Mrs Osman.

3 **Complete the conversation with the sentences (a–d). There is one extra sentence.**

Mrs Osman: Hello, Yasmin. Declan phoned while you were out. ¹ ....

Yasmin: OK. I'll take some dance and hip-hop albums.

Mrs Osman: ² ....

Yasmin: Yes, I know. Did he say how many and what kind?

Mrs Osman: No, he didn't. ³ .... You can ask him yourself.

Yasmin: OK. I'll phone him now.

a He asked me to tell you to take some CDs to the party tomorrow.

b He wants you to phone him back.

c He reminded me to tell you about the party tomorrow.

d He also says you need to buy some party decorations.

4 **Complete the dialogue. Choose the correct option (a, b or c).**

Yasmin: Hi, Declan. It's Yasmin.

Declan: Hi, Yasmin. Did your mum ¹ .... you my message about the party?

Yasmin: Yeah, sure. Don't worry. I've already put a selection of CDs in my bag for tomorrow.

Declan: Great! What about the party decorations?

Yasmin: I'm not sure what to get. What do we need exactly?

Declan: Well, Sara ² .... she wants us ³ .... a big banner that says 'Happy Birthday' on it. We can hang it up at the back of the room, so the twins will see it when they come in.

Yasmin: OK. I can buy one in the supermarket. Anything else?

Declan: She ⁴ .... me to tell you to get some balloons as well.

Yasmin: OK. They sell them in the supermarket too. Who's organising the food?

Declan: Sara is. She's going shopping tomorrow morning. Maybe you could go together.

Yasmin: Good idea. I'll phone her now.

Declan: Oh, can you ⁵ .... buy some plastic cups and plates?

Yasmin: Of course.

Declan: And ⁶ .... her to get a birthday cake as well.

Yasmin: Don't worry. ⁷ ....

1	**a** say	**b** give	**c** remind
2	**a** tells	**b** says	**c** asks
3	**a** to buy	**b** buy	**c** buy her
4	**a** said	**b** says	**c** asked
5	**a** tell her to	**b** to tell her	**c** tell her
6	**a** remind	**b** remember	**c** remember to
7	**a** I remind her	**b** I can	**c** I'll tell her

Pronunciation: words ending in /p/ and /b/, /k/ and /g/, /f/ and /v/

5 ⏺ **7.2** Listen to the sentences (1–6). Circle the words you hear.

1 ⟨lock⟩   log   ⟨leave⟩   live
2 back   bag   cab   cap
3 leaf   leave   off   of
4 half   have   pick   pig
5 pick   pig   cap   cab
6 back   bag   leave   live

Writing: personal news

6 Read Yasmin's email to her friend, Sam. Put the subjects Yasmin talks about (a–d) in the correct order (1–4).

.... **a** a surprise
.... **b** some bad news
.... **c** Sam's birthday
.... **d** the twins' birthday

7 Read the email again and circle the correct options.

┌─────────────────────────────────────┐
● ● ●

Hi Sam,
How was your birthday? Did you do anything to celebrate? Did you get lots of nice presents?

¹ *By the way / Anyway*, it was the twins' birthday yesterday. We organised a party for them and we had a fantastic time. The party was in Declan's garage, which is enormous. Declan's dad let us use his music system. ² *Luckily, / Guess what?* MaxVibe came to the party and sang Happy Birthday to both the twins! ³ *Actually / Anyway*, it wasn't the whole group – just Alesha, the lead singer, but she was amazing. Declan's dad is a sound producer for a record label in London so he knows lots of recording artists. It was a surprise for everyone – even Declan didn't know about it.

My other news is bad news. My brother's flat was burgled last week. ⁴ *Luckily / Unfortunately*, the thieves didn't cause too much damage, but they stole the TV, two computers, the DVD player and the satellite dish!

⁵ *Anyway, / Guess what?* I have to go now and help Declan clear up after the party. We didn't go home until very late last night so the garage is still a mess!

Write soon and tell me all about your birthday.

Love,
Yasmin
└─────────────────────────────────────┘

---

8 Complete the sentences. Choose the correct option (a, b or c).

1 It was Beth's birthday yesterday. ...., it was both Beth and Jenny's birthday – they're twins.
   a Anyway   **b** Actually   **c** Luckily

2 We went walking in the mountains last weekend. ...., it didn't rain.
   a Unfortunately   **b** Luckily   **c** Guess what?

3 Our school had very good exam results this year. ...., I had the best marks in the class in maths!
   a Luckily   **b** Unfortunately   **c** Actually

4 .... We won the national schools citizenship project competition!
   a Luckily   **b** Anyway   **c** Guess what?

5 ...., it's getting late and I'm really tired. I'll write again soon.
   a Anyway   **b** Guess what?   **c** Luckily

9 Write some notes about your own personal news.

Your birthday (party / presents)

News about your family / friends

The best and the worst things at school

Your plans for the summer

10 In your notebook, write an email to your friend with your personal news. Use your ideas from Exercise 9 and include expressions from Exercise 8. Use Yasmin's email to help you.

Reading

1 Match the notes with the writers' purpose. There is one extra purpose.

a to ask for information
b to offer help
c to invite somebody to do something

Hi Declan,
Thanks for a great party. It was fantastic! Would you like to come round to our house on Saturday to play on our new Wii game?
Jenny and Beth

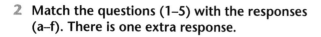

2

Hi Carlos,
We're planning a trip to Spain this summer, but we can't decide which part of Spain to visit. Could you tell me which are the most interesting places to visit? Obviously, we'll come to see you in Barcelona first!
Sara

2 Match the questions (1–5) with the responses (a–f). There is one extra response.

1 Why don't we go to the cinema tonight?
2 Could you explain how this works?
3 Hello Beth. Sara's not home at the moment.
4 I failed one exam this term!
5 We didn't enjoy the concert.

a Yes. Good idea!
b Neither did we.
c That's not so bad.
d I'll tell her.
e Certainly. It's very easy.
f Can you ask her to phone me back?

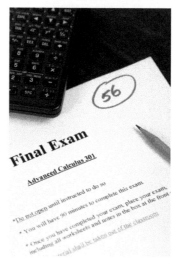

Word list Unit 7

accompany (v)	....
advice (n)	....
ancient (adj)	....
anniversary (n)	....
anxious (adj)	....
anyway (adv)	....
apologise to somebody (phr)	....
apply (v)	....
award (n)	....
be in trouble (phr)	....
behaviour (n)	....
book (n)	....
break the law (phr)	....
burglary (n)	....
burgle (v)	....
by the way (phr)	....
carry out (phr v)	....
charity (n)	....
chef (n)	....
citizen (n)	....
citizenship (n)	....
classmate (n)	....
compete (v)	....
complain (v)	....
confidence (n)	....
counter (n)	....
court (n)	....
customer (n)	....
dedicated (adj)	....
disadvantaged (adj)	....
drop (v)	....
duty (n)	....

encourage (v)	....
face (n)	....
follow (v)	....
get involved (phr)	....
government (n)	....
gun (n)	....
husband (n)	....
ice rink (n)	....
inhabitant (n)	....
key workplace skills (n phr)	....
law (n)	....
leisure centre (n)	....
litter (n)	....
look forward (phr v)	....
luckily (adv)	....
march (n)	....
mess (n)	....
mugging (n)	....
neighbourhood (n)	....
offender (n)	....
order (v)	....
participant (n)	....
pay attention (phr)	....
pick up (phr v)	....
plate (n)	....
platform (n)	....
poster (n)	....
raise (v)	....
record label (n)	....
remind (v)	....
rent (v)	....
respected (adj)	....

robbery (n)	....
shoplifting (n)	....
shout (v)	....
slice (n)	....
smartly-dressed (adj)	....
steal (v)	....
struggle (v)	....
theft (n)	....
thief (n)	....
traffic (n)	....
unemployment (n)	....
unfortunately (adv)	....
unzip (v)	....
victim (n)	....
violence (n)	....
warn (v)	....
whole (v)	....
witness (n)	....
youth (n)	....

U7 Reading Explorer

footstep (n)	....
muddy (adj)	....
pattern (n)	....
powder (n)	....
profile (n)	....
saliva (n)	....
seeds (n pl)	....
shoe print (n)	....
solid (adj)	....
suspect (n)	....
tape (n)	....
tyre track (n)	....
wrapper (n)	....

reporting verbs

Direct speech gives the exact words someone said and uses quotation marks to show this.

Reported speech gives the meaning of what somebody said, but doesn't use all their exact words.

'I like Thai food,' Daisy said. (Direct speech)
Daisy said that she likes Thai food. (Reported speech)

In reported speech, we can use different **reporting verbs** to show how somebody spoke.

Reporting verbs we use in this way include:
advise ask invite order remind tell warn

The pattern with these verbs is **verb + object (+ *not*) + full infinitive**.

'Don't look at the answers,' the teacher said to her students.

*The teacher **told** her students **not to look** at the answers.*

> We usually *invite* or *remind* someone to do something
> We usually *warn* someone not to do something

1 **Choose the correct reporting verbs.**

'Please make yourself at home.'

They *invited / ordered* us to make ourselves at home.

1 'Could you help me, please?'
   She *asked / told* Bobby to help her.
2 'Don't you dare do that again!'
   She *reminded / warned* her not to do that again.
3 'It would be a good idea to stay in bed.'
   The doctor *advised / ordered* Brenda to stay in bed.
4 'Don't forget to take your keys.'
   Mum *told / reminded* me to take my keys.
5 'Don't worry, Dad – I'm OK.'
   Harry *warned / told* his father not to worry.

2 **Rewrite the sentences in reported speech, using reporting verbs from the box. There is one extra verb.**

advise   ask   invite   order   *remind*   tell   warn

'Don't forget to buy some milk,' she said to her husband.
She reminded her husband to buy some milk.

1 'Would you like to go to the mall with me?' Lee said to Aneta.
   ....

2 'Please don't make so much noise,' Mrs Ames said to her son.
   ....

3 'Turn off your mobile in class,' the teacher said to Lauren.
   ....

4 'Get out of the car with your hands up!' the policeman shouted at him.
   ....

5 'You should study every day,' the teacher said to the students.
   ....

There are other reporting verbs which don't follow the pattern of **verb + sb + full infinitive**. These verbs include:

accuse sb of + -ing
*The policeman **accused** him **of stealing** her bag.*

admit + -ing
*He **admitted** stealing her bag.*

apologise for + -ing
*He **apologised for** stealing her bag.*

deny + -ing
*He **denied** stealing her bag.*

describe sth (to sb)
*She **described** her bag.*

offer + full infinitive
*He **offered to carry** her bag.*

refuse + full infinitive
*He **refused to give** her bag back.*

3 **Match what the speakers said (1–5) with the reporting verbs (a–f).**

'The robber was tall and thin,' Alex said to the policeman. *c*

1 'I'll help with the washing up,' Ben said. ......

2 'No, I won't tidy my room!' the boy shouted. ......

3 'I'm sorry I broke your pencil,' Abby said to him. ......

4 'You lost my CD, didn't you?' Diana said to her brother. ......

5 'I didn't borrow your CD,' her brother told her. ......

a *apologise for* + -ing	**d** *offer* + full infinitive
b *accuse* sb *of* + -ing	**e** *refuse* + full infinitive
~~**c** *describe* sth (*to sb*)~~	**f** *deny* + -ing

4 **Rewrite the sentences in Exercise 3 in reported speech, using reporting verbs.**

Alex described the robber to the policeman.

1 ....

2 ....

3 ....

4 ....

5 ....

word order in indirect questions

We can make a statement into a **direct question** by putting a modal, auxiliary or *be* before the subject. If the statement does not have a modal, auxiliary or *be*, we add *do/does/did* before the subject.

Can Jack play the piano?

Is Luke from America?

Does Lee love street dancing?

We can also make direct questions beginning with **question words** such as *What*, *When*, *How*, etc.

What can Jack play?

Where is Luke from?

What does Lee love doing?

5 **Rewrite the sentences as questions, using the question words given.**

The EYP is for <u>young people who are interested in politics</u>.

Who *is the EYP for*?

1 This year's EYP Forum is <u>in Girona, Spain</u>.

Where .... ?

2 People at the Forum will discuss <u>a lot of different subjects</u>.

What .... ?

3 The Forum takes place <u>every summer</u>.

When .... ?

4 This morning's meeting begins <u>at ten o'clock</u>.

What time .... ?

5 Albert's interests include <u>water-polo, acting and politics</u>.

What .... ?

If we add a phrase such as *I don't know, I'm not sure* or *I wonder* in front of a direct question, then it becomes an **indirect statement**. The word order is, **subject** + **modal/auxiliary** (if there is one) + **verb**.

*What **can Jack** play?*

*I don't know what **Jack can** play.*

If the direct question does not begin with a question word, we use the word *if* in the indirect statement.

Can Jack play the piano?

*I don't know **if** Jack can play the piano.*

We can make a direct question more polite by using a phrase such as *Can/Could you tell me ... ?* or *Do you know ... ?* at the beginning. The original direct question is now an **indirect question**. These begin with a question word or *if*.

*Where **is the post office**?*

*Do you know where **the post office is**?*

*How much **does this** weigh?*

*Can you tell me how much **this** weighs?*

*Is **this** lecture hall 3?*

*Could you tell me if **this is** lecture hall 3?*

6 **Rewrite the direct questions as indirect statements or indirect questions.**

Which room is the meeting in?

Did anyone tell you *which room the meeting is in?*

1 How do we get to the Forum from here?

I'm not sure ....

2 Are you going to sing at the concert?

Have you decided ...... ?

3 Can we get extra copies of the programme?

Could you please tell me ...... ?

4 What time is the lunch break?

Does anyone know ...... ?

5 Do they plan to go to next year's Forum?

I wonder ....

8A Survival

Vocabulary: holidays

adventure holiday	beach holiday	cruise
foreign holiday	package holiday	safari
sightseeing holiday	trekking	

1 Match the descriptions (1–8) with the holidays in the box.

1 It was very exciting being in a different country! Communicating wasn't a problem because most people spoke a bit of English. ....

2 I wouldn't like to spend so much time at sea. I think it would be boring. ....

3 We travelled by jeep through the jungle and saw some amazing wildlife. ....

4 Our holiday was very relaxing. We spent our time sunbathing and swimming in the sea. ....

5 A group of twenty people set off to cross the Vilcabamba mountain range in Peru. They were going to climb Mount Salkantay and follow the Inca Trail to Machu Picchu. ....

6 We travelled to Rome and Pompeii to see the historic buildings and monuments. ....

7 Everything was included in the price – the food, the accommodation, the flight and the airport transfers. ....

8 We went rafting down rivers, climbed mountains and learned to survive in the wild. ....

2 Circle the correct option.

1 We stayed in a different *hotel / hostel* every night. It was OK, but we had to share a room with other walkers.

2 The *day trip / eco-tour* was really interesting. We visited the museum in the morning and spent the afternoon looking round the city.

3 The *theme park / adventure holiday* was great. The kids sailed pirate ships, saw their favourite adventure heroes and went on a huge roller coaster.

4 In Brazil, we went on an *eco-tour / adventure holiday* to the Amazon jungle where we went trekking in the jungle. We stayed with local families and spent two days tree planting as part of a local conservation project.

5 The *hotel / family* organised lots of activities for the children so that parents could relax by the pool or have a peaceful meal in the restaurant.

6 It was a great place for *retired / young* couples because there weren't any bars or discos.

Vocabulary: holiday packing

3 Read the clues and complete the crossword.

Across

2 You'll need one of these if you're going in the sea.

5 You can carry it on your back and you can sleep in it.

7 You pack this before you go on holiday.

8 It's useful for peeling fruit, cutting things or opening tins.

Down

1 It contains medicine and bandages. (3 words)

3 You should take them in case it rains.

4 You get inside this when you want to go to bed. (2 words)

5 You use it when you're camping so that you can see in the dark.

6 You carry this on your back.

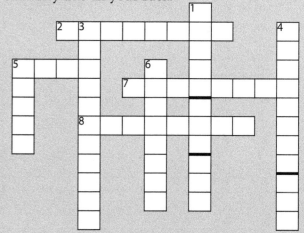

Grammar: second conditional

4 Match the beginnings of the sentences (1–6) with the endings (a–g). There is one extra ending.

1 If I went on a cruise,
2 If you went to live in a foreign country,
3 What would you do
4 Would Alberto teach me Italian if
5 I'd probably travel round the world
6 If we went to the theme park,

a I asked him?
b I think everyone would have a great time.
c would you learn the language first?
d if you became ill on holiday?
e I'd tell the police.
f I wouldn't get seasick.
g if I had enough money.

5 Complete the second conditional sentences with the correct form of the verbs in brackets.

1 If I .... (go) on holiday in Canada, I .... (visit) Niagra Falls.
2 .... (you / scream) if you .... (find) a snake in your tent?
3 What .... (you / do) if you .... (meet) a brown bear?
4 I .... (not / run). If I .... (run), the bear .... (chase) me.
5 If you .... (have) a lot of money, where .... (you / go) on holiday?
6 I .... (lend) Sarah my rucksack if she .... (want) to borrow it.

6 Write second conditional questions and statements.

1 If / your family / win / holiday / Florida, / what / you / do?
....

2 If / my little sister / come / too, / we / have to / go / Disney World.
....

3 What / you / say / if / you / meet / Mickey Mouse?
....

4 If / he / speak / me, / I / feel / embarrassed.
....

5 What / you / do / if / you / not like / Disney World?
....

6 If / my sister / not mind, / we / visit / Miami.
....

Working with words: adjective ➔ adverb

7 Complete the table. Write opposite adjectives and adverbs.

Adjective	Adverb	Opposite adjective	Opposite adverb
careful	*carefully*	*careless*	
easy			
good			
loud			
lucky			
fast			

8 Complete the sentences with adjectives and adverbs from Exercise 7.

1 If we run ...., we might catch the train.
2 There are lots of road accidents because people don't pay enough attention on the road and drive ....
3 I can't hear you. Everyone is talking very ....
4 My sister fell off her bike. ...., she wasn't hurt.
5 Our team won the match .... The final score was 6–0.

9 Complete the text with the words in the box.

calm	carefully	early
good	hard	late
loudly	quickly	well

Philippa stayed up [1] .... last night. She was studying [2] .... for her exams the next day. The next morning she didn't hear her alarm at 7 o'clock, even though it rang [3] .... At about 8 o'clock her mother woke her up. Philippa dressed [4] .... and ran downstairs. Her mother was making toast. 'I'll drive you to school today,' she said. 'Now, make sure you have a [5] .... breakfast.' Philippa ate two large slices of toast and drank some orange juice. Then, her mother took her to school. When she went into the exam hall, Philippa felt [6] .... and relaxed. She read the instructions [7] .... and finished the exam [8] .... When she arrived home she was smiling and told her mum: 'I think I did [9] .... in the exams. Perhaps it was the breakfast you gave me!'

Reading

1 **Look at the photos. Tick (✓) the things you can see.**

beach ☐   columns ☐   entrance hall ☐
ice ☐   igloo ☐   diver ☐   tropical fish ☐

2 **Read the article and match the photos (a–b) with the texts (1–2).**

3 **Choose the best heading for each text. There is one extra heading.**

a A family skiing trip
b A holiday under the sea
c A winter wonderland

4 **Read the article again. Read the summary sentences below and decide who said them. Tick (✓) the boxes.**

	Emma	Luke	Both
1 My parents wouldn't let me stay at home.	☐	☐	☐
2 I didn't know anything about the holiday.	☐	☐	☐
3 I wanted to find something special for them.	☐	☐	☐
4 When we arrived, I was really surprised.	☐	☐	☐
5 My parents did a lot of things on their own.	☐	☐	☐
6 I made friends with other people my age.	☐	☐	☐
7 I spent a lot of time with my parents.	☐	☐	☐

Cool holidays with your parents

Cool holidays with your parents? Yes, it is possible! Two teenagers wrote to tell us about their fantastic experiences on holiday with mum and dad.

1 ....

If you had to go on a winter holiday with your parents, where would you go? Last January, it was my parents' twentieth wedding anniversary. They wanted to go on a family holiday to celebrate and told us to choose the best place. We wanted to surprise them with something different. A few days later, we found the perfect place: the Ice Hotel in Québec. We booked it immediately.

When we arrived at the hotel three months later, we couldn't believe our eyes. The entrance hall had huge columns and chandeliers made of ice. It was really amazing! In fact, everything in the hotel was made from snow and ice, including the walls, the floors, the furniture, and even the plates and glasses in the bar! Because the hotel is in the middle of a huge winter resort, my sister and I could go skiing and snowboarding every day. Mum and dad had a great time too. They went for walks and went shopping in the village. They even went snowmobiling! We made friends with other teenagers at the hotel. In the evenings, we met them in the ice café while mum and dad relaxed in the ice bar.
Emma, USA

2 ....

Summer holidays with mum and dad usually mean hot sunshine, sandy beaches and being bored! Last year, I was sixteen and I told them I didn't want to go on holiday with them. They understood why, but they weren't happy about it and said I had to go with them. I was really annoyed! I didn't talk to them about the holiday again.

Three months later, we were at the airport and boarding a plane for Florida. 'Where are we going?' I asked. 'I'm too old for Disney World!' They told me it was a surprise – and they were right! We spent five days learning to scuba-dive in Key Largo. Then we spent two nights in the Jules Verne Lodge. This has to be the coolest hotel in the world! It's an underwater laboratory, but there is also accommodation for guests. We had to dive down to get to the entrance. Inside, there was a common room with views of the lagoon. The marine biologists told us all about the tropical fish and then we went out diving with experts to see things for ourselves. It really was the most fantastic holiday, and I had a great time with my parents!
Luke, UK

Grammar: quantifiers + adjectives

5 **Complete the text with the words in the box.**

bit	had	if	lot	much	very	were

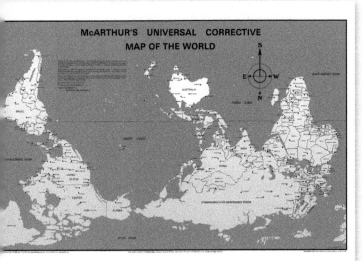

What would you do ¹..................... someone gave you a copy of this map? Would you say it was upside-down? Would you think it was funny? Although this map is ² .... different to most maps, it is actually a real map. It's also ³ .... more interesting than normal maps. Australia is at the top and Europe is on the edge of the map. If you ⁴ .... Indonesian, you would probably like this map, because Indonesia in the centre. The map was created by an Australian called Stuart McArthur. It is called McArthur's Universal Corrective Map. It is also known as the South-Up map. When Stuart McArthur was twelve years old, he drew his first upside-down map for a geography project. His teacher just told him to do it again. When he was fifteen, some exchange students from the USA said that he was from the bottom of the world. This comment was a ⁵ .... unkind and, of course, it wasn't true. In 1979, when he was at university, McArthur published the first, modern, upside-down map. His map has been a ⁶ .... more successful than anyone imagined, and has sold 350,000 copies.
So, what do you think? If you ⁷ .... a copy of this map on your wall, would you see the world differently?

Listening

6 **8.1** **Listen to three conversations. Match the speakers (1–3) with the holidays (a–d). There is one extra holiday.**

Speaker 1	**a** package holiday
Speaker 2	**b** sailing
Speaker 3	**c** sightseeing
	d trekking

7 **Listen again and answer the questions.**

Conversation 1
1 Why has the woman got backache?
2 Where do the couple plan to stay tomorrow?

Conversation 2
3 Where is the bridge?
4 When was the bridge built?

Conversation 3
5 What time does the flight leave?
6 Where will the couple eat their evening meal?

Vocabulary: transport

8 **Circle the odd one out.**

1 the underground   ship   ferry   hovercraft
2 camel   horse   mountain bike   canoe
3 catamaran   jeep   van   taxi
4 plane   helicopter   balloon   tram
5 the underground   lorry   tram   train
6 canoe   tractor   catamaran   ferry

9 **Complete the sentences with the correct form of the words from Exercise 8.**

1 A .... floats on a cushion of air.
2 If you went on a safari, you'd probably travel in a ....
3 You can take your car on the .... from England to France.
4 My dad is a carpenter. He needs his .... to transport things in.
5 Big .... take things from the factory to the shops.
6 South American Indians still use .... to travel along the river.

Working with words: verb + noun

10 **Choose the correct option (a, b or c).**

1 You can .... a tractor when you're fourteen.
  a ride   **b** drive   **c** take
2 I usually .... the bus to school.
  a take   **b** drive   **c** go
3 We .... round the coast on a catamaran.
  a flew   **b** sailed   **c** drove
4 The trekkers .... lost in the mountains.
  a went   **b** spent   **c** got
5 We .... a lovely meal in the hotel restaurant.
  a spent   **b** had   **c** got
6 I enjoy .... my motorbike.
  a going   **b** getting   **c** riding

Useful expressions

1 Complete the useful expressions with words in the box.

> could   don't   I   I'd   should   you'll   would

1 ……….. you give us the key to our room, please?

2 Don't leave the room later than 10 o'clock or ……….. have to pay extra.

3 If I were you, ……….. wait at the reception desk.

4 What can ……….. do for you?

5 Why ……….. you phone room service?

6 ……….. you like me to give her a message?

7 That's terrible! You ……….. complain to the manager.

2 Read the dialogues. For each function (a–e) write the number of the example sentence (1–7). Some functions have more than one example.

R = Receptionist, G = Guest

R: [1] Good afternoon. What can I do for you?

G: [2] Could you tell me where the restaurant is, please?

R: [3] Yes, of course. Go to the end of the corridor and turn right. Don't turn left or you'll be in the kitchens!

G: What's the best way to get to the cathedral?

R: [4] If I were you, I'd catch the number 10 bus and then walk.

G: I think my bag has been stolen from my room!

R: [5] You should talk to the manager.

G: Excuse me. My sister has hurt her leg and our room is on the second floor.

R: [6] Why don't you use the lift. It's just over there.

R: [7] Would you like the porter to carry your suitcase for you?

G: Yes, please. It's quite heavy.

a offering help

……………………………………………….

b making a suggestion

……………………………………………….

c requesting information

……………………………………………….

d giving instructions

……………………………………………….

e giving advice

……………………………………………….

3 Complete the dialogues. Use the useful expressions in Exercise 1 and the dialogue in Exercise 2 to help you.

G = Guest, H = Hotel porter, R = Receptionist

a G: Excuse me, where's room 301?

H: It's on the third floor. I'd take the lift, [1] ……………….. .

G: It's not working.

H: Oh, [2] ……………….. help with your bags?

G: Yes, please.

b G: My bag has been stolen! What [3] ……………. I do?

R: If I were you, [4] ……………….. go to the police station. It's just down the road.

c G: Excuse me?

R: Yes, what [5] ……………….. do for you?

G: Where can I get something to eat?

R: Hmm, it's very late. I'm afraid the restaurant is closed now. Why [6] ……………….. phone for a pizza?

4 Match the sentences (1–5) with the responses (a–f). There is one extra response.

1 Could I have the key to Room 16, please?

2 Let's eat at the Riverside Restaurant next week.

3 Where can we get a taxi to the city centre?

4 What should we do if the weather's nice tomorrow?

5 What's the best way to get to the beach from the hotel?

a Why don't you go on a river trip?

b Good idea. We should book a table as soon as possible.

c Yes, certainly. Here you are.

d Take a bus. I wouldn't walk if I were you. It's quite a long way.

e Yes. It's on the first floor.

f Would you like me to order one for you?

5 8.2 Listen and complete the information.

Hilltop Farm Campsite

Name: [1] ………………..
Number of tents: [2] ………………..
Number of campers: [3] ………………..
Location of tent: bottom [4] ………………..
                       plot number [5] ………………..
Cost: [6] ……………….. per person
                       [7] ……………….. per tent

Pronunciation: difficult words

6 **Read the sentences aloud with a partner. How do you pronounce the underlined words?**

1 Would you like some coffee and <u>biscuits</u>?
2 The ship was <u>comfortable</u> and the sea was calm.
3 Can you see the <u>castle</u> on top of the <u>mountain</u>?
4 What's the <u>answer</u> to this question?
5 He's going on a <u>business</u> trip tomorrow.
6 When you travel to a <u>foreign</u> country, you have to go <u>through</u> passport control.
7 Those two <u>women</u> are chefs in a famous restaurant.

7 **8.3 Listen, check your pronunciation and repeat.**

Writing: holiday tips

8 **Read Kylie's email about a camping trip. Tick (✓) the things she mentions.**

camping equipment ☐   certificates ☐
food ☐   passports ☐   sleeping bags ☐
tents ☐   the weather ☐
what clothes to bring ☐

9 **Complete the email with *in case, or* and *unless*.**

```
 ○○○                                             ⬭

Hi Lucy,
Are you still coming camping with us this weekend? I
hope so! I'm sure it'll be great fun.
We're busy organising the camping gear at the
moment. My dad's cleaning the tents and my mum's
washing all the picnic things – they were a bit dusty
after being in the cupboard for a year! Did I tell you
that there's a lake and an activities centre near the
campsite. I'm taking my canoeing and swimming
certificates ¹ .................... we need to show
them to somebody. Bring your swimsuit as well,
² .................... you won't be able to go swimming if it
gets really hot.
Also, mum says you'll need to bring a sleeping bag,
³ .................... you want to use my brother's old one.
I wouldn't use it if I were you – he probably hasn't
washed it for years! What else? It's a good idea to
bring your waterproofs ⁴ .................... it rains. We've
got lots of camping equipment, so I don't think you
need anything else, ⁵ .................... you want to bring
your own torch for going out at night.
Anyway, let me know if you're still want to come
with us!
Kylie
```

10 **Write the second sentence so that it means the same as the first sentence. Use *in case, or* and *unless*.**

1 Remember your swimsuit, if you want to swim in the lake.
   Remember your swimsuit ....
   .... able to swim in the lake.

2 Bring your own sleeping bag if you don't want to use my brother's.
   You can use my brother's sleeping bag
   .... your own.

3 Bring your walking boots because we might go trekking.
   Bring your walking boots ....
   ....

4 You'll need a torch so that you can see in the dark.
   Don't forget your torch ....
   .... able to see in the dark.

5 If the weather forecast is correct, it will be hot and sunny.
   The weather is going to be hot and sunny
   .... wrong.

11 **Match the words in the box with the holidays (1–5). You can use the words more than once.**

| camera   gloves   guidebook   hat |
| insect repellent   novel   passport   rucksack |
| sandals   ski jacket   socks   sun cream |
| sunglasses   swimming trunks   swimsuit   torch |
| towel   travel tablets   walking boots   waterproofs |

1 skiing holiday:
   ....
2 sightseeing:
   ....
3 beach holiday:
   ....
4 safari:
   ....
5 cruise:
   ....

12 **Choose one of the holidays from Exercise 11 and add two more things to the list.**

13 **You have invited a friend to come on holiday with you. Write an email to tell him or her what to bring. Use the ideas in Exercises 10 and 11.**

Reading

1 Match the signs (a–d) with the places (1–5). There is one extra place.

a

Danger!
Do not swim
when the red
flag
is flying

b

Day trip
to Water World
theme park!
Please enquire at
the desk for
information

c

To book your low cost flights, click below.

Reserve now

d

Departure gates 11–23 →

Duty-free shopping →

Toilets ↑

1 on a beach   ....
2 at an airport   ....
3 on a website   ....
4 at a swimming pool   ....
5 in a hotel   ....

Listening

2 Listen and answer the questions.

1 *8.4* Listen to the answerphone message. Where is it from?
  a a travel agent's
  b a shop
  c a hotel

2 *8.5* Listen to the announcement. Where is it?
  a at a train station
  b at an airport
  c on a plane

3 *8.6* Listen to the conversation. Where are the people?
  a on a train
  b on a plane
  c on a bus

4 *8.7* Listen to the announcement. Where is it?
  a at an airport
  b at an underground station
  c at a bus station

Word list Unit 8

accident (n)	....
adventure (n)	....
adventurous (adj)	....
announcement (n)	....
arrangement (n)	....
at first (phr)	....
board (n)	....
beach (n)	....
calmly (adj)	....
camping gear (n)	....
canoe (n)	....
carpenter (n)	....
challenge (n)	....
chandelier (n)	....
chase (v)	....
climb (v)	....
coastline (n)	....
common sense (n)	....
cool-headed (adj)	....
cruise (n)	....
cushion of air (n)	....
destination (n)	....
dusty (adj)	....
edge (n)	....
employment (n)	....
enquire (inquire) (v)	....
entrance hall (n)	....
expedition (n)	....
explorer (n)	....
ferry (n)	....
first aid kit (n)	....
float (v)	....
foreign (adj)	....
gear (n)	....
get lost (phr v)	....

get seasick (v phr)	....
glove (n)	....
guidebook (n)	....
harmless (v)	....
hike (v)	....
hovercraft (n)	....
immediately (adv)	....
in case (phr)	....
industry (n)	....
jellyfish (n)	....
journey (n)	....
knowledgeable (adj)	....
lagoon (n)	....
landmark (n)	....
lift (n)	....
lorry (n)	....
loudly (adv)	....
luggage (n)	....
luxury (adj)	....
package holiday (n)	....
paradise (n)	....
patiently (adv)	....
pedalo (n)	....
penknife (n)	....
pleased (adj)	....
porter (n)	....
print (v)	....
realize (v)	....
retire (v)	....
retired (adj)	....
roller coaster (n)	....
rucksack (n)	....
safely (adj)	....
sail (v)	....
set off (phr v)	....

shallow (adj)	....
sightseeing (n)	....
sleeping bag (n)	....
snowmobile (n)	....
sunbathing (n)	....
sunrise (n)	....
survival (n)	....
swimming trunks (n)	....
swimsuit (n)	....
tap water (n)	....
torch (n)	....
tough (adj)	....
towel (n)	....
tram (n)	....
travel sick (n)	....
trek (v)	....
underground (n)	....
unkind (adj)	....
unless (conj)	....
upside-down (adj)	....
valid (adj)	....
waterproofs (n)	....
U8 Reading Explorer	
fuel (n)	....
grassland (n)	....
herd (v)	....
inquisitive (adj)	....
limited (adj)	....
log cabin (n)	....
manatee (n)	....
marked footpath (n)	....
palm (n)	....
piranha (n)	....
reindeer (n)	....
thrive (v)	....

Grammar Practice | Unit 8

Second conditional

We use the **second conditional** to talk about imaginary actions or results which depend on an imaginary condition in the present or future.

*If he **was** a movie star, he'**d be** rich and famous.*

We form the second conditional with *If* + **past simple** for the condition, followed by *would/wouldn't* + **bare infinitive** for the resulting action or situation. We do not use *would* for the condition.

*If **I was** in a foreign country (condition), I'**d learn** the language (result).*

*I **wouldn't do** well at school (result) if **I didn't** study (condition).*

If + **past simple** = imaginary, in the present/future.

1 Choose the correct words.

I was / I'd be very scared if I would be / was all alone in the jungle at night.

1 If someone *was / would be* with me, it *wouldn't be / wasn't* so bad.

2 I *tried / I'd try* to light a fire if it *got / would get* cold.

3 If I *was / I'd be* able to stay awake, I *didn't sleep / wouldn't sleep* all night.

4 If *I'd hear / I heard* a wild animal, *I'd keep / I kept* very quiet.

5 If I *saw / would see* a snake, I *killed / I'd kill* it.

2 Complete the second conditional sentences with the correct tense and form of the verbs in brackets.

I'*d call* (call) Joanna on her mobile if I *had* (have) her number.

1 If I ...... (know) the solution to your problem I ...... (help) you.

2 Theresa ...... (have) a lot more friends if she ...... (not be) so selfish.

3 If my best friend ...... (tell) me a secret I ...... (not say) a word to anyone else.

4 I ...... (watch) TV tonight if I ...... (not have to) study for tomorrow's test.

5 If we ...... (not wear) a school uniform, some students ...... (feel) embarrassed about not having expensive clothes.

3 Write sentences and questions in the second conditional with these words.

If you / be lost / in the desert, what / you / do?

If you were lost in the desert, what would you do?

1 It / be / wonderful if we / be able to / fly like birds.

....

2 If I / plan / to visit another country, I / read / lots of information about it first.

....

3 If you / rule / the world, how / you / make / it a better place?

....

4 If I / be / you, I / talk / to the teacher about the problem.

....

5 If you / fail / your driving test, / you / try / again?

....

6 If I / be / a really good footballer like my brother, I / play / professionally.

....

would

Would has the same form for all subjects and is followed by the **bare infinitive**. In the affirmative, we almost always use the short form (*I'd, you'd, he'd,* etc). The negative of **would** is **wouldn't** *(would not)*.

We make questions by putting **Would** before the subject, and then the bare infinitive of the main verb. In short answers we use **would** or **wouldn't**. We don't use the main verb.

We can also make questions using **question words**.

***What** would you do if your car broke down?*

Apart from the result clause in second conditional sentences, we use **would** for:

- imaginary situations
  *It **would** be nice to have a lot of money.*

- polite offers and invitations
  ***Would** you like me to help you?*

- polite requests
  ***Would** you pass me the salt, please?*

- giving advice
  *It **wouldn't** be a good idea to do that.*

4 Write sentences and questions using *would*.

you / like / go / to the cinema tonight?

Would you like to go to the cinema tonight?

1 I / not do / that if I / be / you.

....

2 It / be / great if we / go / on holiday together.

....

3 you / open / the door for me, please?

....

4 a trip to India / be / very exciting.

....

5 you / feel / lonely if you / be / an only child?

....

very, really, quite, a bit, a lot, much + adjectives

We can add a word such as *very*, *really*, *quite*, etc. to the adjective to quantify an adjective.

Playing the guitar is quite difficult, but playing the violin is very difficult.

- *very*, *really*, *quite*, *a bit* + adjective
- *a bit* + adjective is used only with adjectives that suggest a negative feeling
- *much, a lot, a bit* + comparative adjective (*-er, more/less*)
- *a bit* + comparative adjective is used with all adjectives that suggest a negative or a positive feeling

5 **Choose the correct words.**

Flying there would be ~~very~~ / *much* faster than going by train.

1 This trip would be *really / a lot* boring if my friend wasn't with me.

2 It's also *quite / much* hot and uncomfortable on the train.

3 I suppose it would be *quite / a bit* easier if we didn't have to carry so much equipment.

4 Flying is actually *quite / a lot* safer than travelling by train in my country.

5 The scenery is *very / a bit* beautiful too.

unless, in case and or

Unless, *in case* and *or* are used in first conditional sentences. We have seen the most common pattern of first conditional, which is **If + present ... future**

If it rains tomorrow, we'll stay at home.

- *Unless* follows this common pattern, but it means **if + negative**.
  You'll miss your flight if you don't hurry.
  = *You'll miss your flight unless you hurry.*

- *In case* means *because this might happen*; it goes in the place of the *if + present simple* clause. It can also follow the imperative.
  I'll take my coat because it might get cold.
  = *I'll take my coat in case it gets cold.*

- *Or* means *if the opposite happens*; it usually follows the imperative and it replaces the whole *If + present simple* clause and is followed by *will*.
  Be careful. If you aren't careful, you'll make a mistake.
  = *Be careful or you'll make a mistake.*

6 **Complete the sentences with *unless, or* or *in case*.**

Your trip will take about four hours *unless* there's heavy traffic.

1 Don't drive too fast ...... you'll have an accident.

2 I'll make some sandwiches ...... you get hungry on the motorway.

3 You won't need to stop at all ...... you have some kind of emergency.

4 I'll lend you a road map ...... you lose your way.

5 Take your mobile ...... you won't be able to call us when you get there.

7 **Complete each second sentence so it means the same as the first sentence or pair of sentences. Use *unless, or* or *in case*.**

It might rain, so bring an umbrella.

Bring *an umbrella in case it rains*.

1 Stop doing that! If you don't stop, I'll get really angry!

Stop ....

2 If his flight isn't delayed, he'll arrive at half past ten.

He'll arrive ....

3 Remember to use sun cream. If you forget, you'll get sunburn.

Don't forget to ....

4 You might have to wait around at the airport, so take a book to read.

Take a book ....

5 We won't go to the beach if it isn't really hot.

We won't ....

Grammar: reporting verbs

1 **Report the guide's words. Use the words in brackets.**

1 'Please be quiet, everyone.' (ask)

He ....

2 'Would anyone like to ask any questions?' (invite / the visitors)

He ....

3 'Don't touch the sculptures!' (warn / the visitors)

He ....

4 'You mustn't take any photographs.' (tell / us)

He ....

5 'There's a café and souvenir shop on the second floor.' (say)

He ....

6 'Don't forget to be back on the bus at five o'clock.' (remind)

He ....

2 marks per item: ...... / 12 marks

2 **What did the people say? Complete the sentences.**

1 She warned him not to do that again.

'You ....

2 We invited them to come in and take their coats off.

'Please come ....

3 She reminded me to go to my music lesson at 3.30.

'Don't ....

4 She ordered him to take his hands out of his pockets and open his jacket.

'Take ....

5 She asked me how much a new MP3 player costs.

'How ....

2 marks per item: ...... / 10 marks

3 **Put the words in order to make indirect questions.**

1 can / is, / tell / me / the / where / you / please? / station

....

2 printer / explain / you / could / works? / how / this

....

3 you / could / costs? / me / how / this /coat / much / tell

....

4 this / anybody / know / stops / if / bus / at / the / does / shopping centre?

....

5 if / can / tell / you / train / me / a / leaving / there / tonight? / for / is / Paris

....

1 mark per item: ..... / 5 marks

4 **Write sentences and questions with the second conditional.**

1 If I .... (have) a lot of money, I .... (buy) a big sailing boat.

2 Which countries .... (you / visit) first if .... (sail) around the world?

3 I .... (go) to the Galapagos islands if I .... (can) get permission.

4 What .... (you / do) if .... (feel) ill in the middle of the ocean?

5 If I .... (be) seriously ill, I .... (call) for a doctor to fly out.

6 .... (you / take) me with you, if I .... (learn) how to sail?

2 marks per item: ..... / 12 marks

5 **Circle the correct option.**

1 I would *really / very* love to visit South America.

2 I think swimming with sharks would be *quite / much* exciting.

3 Foreign holidays are *more / much* cheaper than before.

4 I think New York is *a lot / very* more dangerous than Tokyo.

5 Sometimes it's *a bit / more* faster to walk than take the underground!

1 mark per item: ..... / 5 marks

Easily confused words

6 **Complete the text with the words in the box.**

| hers | mine | ours | There | There's | yours |

When Steve and I arrived in Mumbai, the bus driver threw everyone's luggage off the bus.

[1] .... were lots of bags and suitcases. Two of them were [2] ....

'Which bags are [3] ....?' asked our guide, Sanjay.

'This big, red one is [4] ....,' said Steve.

'What about your girlfriend's bag? Which one is [5] ....?' asked Sanjay.

'It's the blue rucksack,' I answered.

Sanjay picked up our bags and pointed to an old VW Polo.' [6] .... my car,' he said.

1 mark per item: ..... / 6 marks

Vocabulary: cities and towns

7 Read the definitions and write the words.

1 a place where you can look at paintings
a..................... g.....................

2 buildings where many people work
o..................... b.....................

3 teenagers can go here in their free time
y..................... c.....................

4 a place where you can watch a football match
s .... s.....................

5 travel services that everyone can use
p .... t ....

6 writing on public buildings   g.....................

7 cars, buses and lorries on the road
t.....................

8 you shouldn't drop it in the street
l.....................

9 destroying public property   v.....................

10 groups of young people who meet on the street   g.....................

1 mark per item: ...... / 10 marks

Adjectives and adverbs

8 Circle the correct option.

1 You *stole / robbed* my jacket!

2 No I didn't. I just *borrowed / lent* it.

3 Were there any witnesses at the crime *scene / scenery*?

4 This *woman / women* saw exactly what happened.

5 They were arrested for *mugging / stealing* a woman outside the railway station.

1 mark per item: ..... / 5 marks

9 Complete the sentences with an adjective or an adverb.

1 Kim's parents are from China so he speaks Chinese and English really ....

2 My dad sings .... in the shower. Even the neighbours can hear him.

3 The thief was .... and left a lot of evidence for the police.

4 The holiday ended ....We missed the plane home and lost our luggage!

5 It isn't .... to drink tap water in Sri Lanka.

6 David is quite .... He hates waiting.

7 The guide spoke very .... and we couldn't always hear what she was saying.

8 The desert is a .... place. If you got lost, you wouldn't survive for very long.

1 mark per item: ..... / 8 marks

Travel and holidays

10 Complete the sentences with the correct piece of survival equipment.

1 Trekkers use a .... to show where north is.

2 Mike got very wet because he forgot his ....

3 I used my .... to cut it. It's very sharp.

4 It's important to take a good .... in case people hurt themselves.

5 We used the .... to plan our route.

1 mark per item: ..... / 5 marks

11 Choose the correct option.

1 In the UK you can ride a *motorbike / car* when you're seventeen.

2 Have you ever *flown / driven* a helicopter?

3 What time *are / is* the news on?

4 When is Jade *coming / going* back from her holiday?

5 We *had / got* lunch in a café outside.

6 My dad *got / went* lost while he was driving.

7 My dad *spends / passes* a lot of time in the garden.

8 I always wear sun cream *unless / in case* it's very cloudy.

1 mark per item: ..... / 8 marks

12 Complete the dialogue with one word each gap.

Receptionist: Good evening. What
[1] .... for you?

Guest: We're very hungry, and the restaurant is closed.

Receptionist: [2] .... you order a sandwich from room service?

Guest: I've already phoned the number but there's no answer.

Receptionist: [3] .... like me to call them? I think there's a problem with the phone. If I [4] ...., I'd go to the kitchen and talk to the chef.

Guest: I disagree. Actually, I think you [5] .... talk to the chef. I'm the guest!

1 mark per item: ...... / 10 marks

Leaving and taking messages

13 Match the questions (1–4) with the answers (a–d).

1 Can I speak to Annie, please?

2 Can you give her a message, please?

3 What's the message?

4 Can you tell her to phone me back?

a Can you remind her to bring our project to school tomorrow?

b I'm afraid Annie's out at the moment.

c Of course. I'll tell her to call you.

d Yes, of course.

1 mark per item: ..... / 4 marks

Total marks: ..... / 100

High school graduation

Read about high school graduation in three different countries. Match the photographs (a–c) with the countries (1–3) below. Write the correct country headings for each text.

1 Japan   ....
2 North America ....
3 Norway   ....

a

For many teenagers around the world, graduating from high school is a big event. In most countries, schools organise a *graduation* ceremony or traditional dances to celebrate.

1 ....

For high school students in this country, graduation is the most important time of their lives. Before graduation, students and teachers *decorate* the school with pictures and photographs, coloured lights and *ribbons*. *The graduation ceremony* is often outside in the school grounds or on the athletics field and students invite their friends and family to the ceremony. The graduates usually wear a *cap* and gown – a long, black coat and a square hat with a *tassel*. At the beginning of the ceremony, the students *line up* in alphabetical order. The band begins to play and the students *march* in. There are a lot of *speeches* and then the principal reads out each graduate's name. The event is sometimes quiet and serious, but sometimes the people in the audience *cheer* loudly and blow *horns*. At the end of the ceremony, the students throw their caps and confetti in the air.

At the end of the school year, there is also a formal dance, called the senior prom. Boys and girls wear very formal clothes. The girls wear traditional dresses and the boys wear *tuxedos* and a tie. Girls often spend a lot of money on their prom dresses. Sometimes, a group of friends rents a limousine to take them to the prom. Many boys and girls take *a date*. When this happens, the boy gives the girl some flowers to wear on her dress. At the prom, there is usually a live band, a dinner and lots of dancing. At the end of the evening, the best couple are *crowned* the king and queen of the prom.

2 ....

The school year finishes in February when students take their final exams and graduation is usually in April. In the school hall, or gym, the walls are decorated with special *curtains*. All the students in the school go to the ceremony. Not many parents come to the graduation ceremony – only some mothers. In most schools, the graduates wear their school uniform.

When the audience are in their seats, the ceremony begins. The school's brass band plays a classical march and the graduates walk into the hall and sit down. The school principal reads out different *announcements* and the students have to stand up, *bow* and sit down again. Then everyone sings the school song. After that, the class tutors read out the names of each student. The students say 'hai' (yes) when they hear their name. They receive their diplomas and the principal makes a long speech, usually about *patience* and hard work. After the ceremony, the students stay in the school. While they are walking around, they say goodbye to their favourite teachers and remember all the good times. They smile and bow a lot and sometimes they cry, as well.

b

3.....................

High schools in this country are similar to schools in most parts of Europe. There is usually a graduation ceremony inside the school and a formal dance. However, students who are going to university when they leave school also take part in another *tradition*. At the beginning of May, they all put on long *overalls* with sleeves, or dungarees. These overalls are blue if they are going to study economics and red if they are going to study an *arts and humanities* subject. Students of medicine wear white and engineering students wear black. They wear the same clothes every day for the next two weeks and don't wash them.

The students also paint cars and buses the same colour as their overalls, and go out into the street to party. This tradition is called 'russ' or 'russefeiring'. The word comes from the red (russ) caps that the students all wear. Students often give each other cards with their photo and contact *details* on them. The photo is usually funny and has a funny caption written under it. The russefeiring starts on 1 May and finishes on 17 May, the Norwegian national day. The students are an important and colourful part of the national day celebrations.

c

In which country (or countries) ...

1 do students wear their school uniform on graduation day?
....

2 do students wear different-coloured clothes?
....

3 does the principal give a speech to all the students in the school?
....

4 do students join a national celebration?
....

5 does the graduation ceremony take place outside?
....

6 do students wear the same clothes for two weeks?
....

7 do they also have a formal dance?
....

8 do the girls wear expensive dresses?
....

9 do graduates march in to the sound of a band?
....

10 do they invite relatives and friends to the ceremony?
....

11 do future university students celebrate in the street?
....

12 do students sing the school song?
....

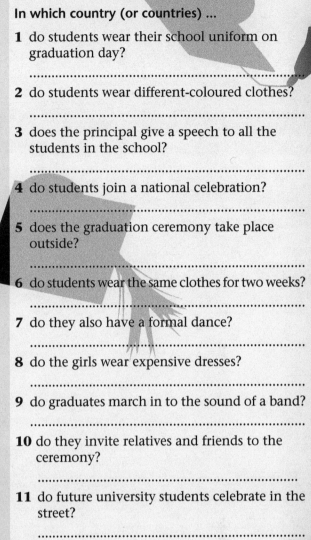

Answers:
Photos
1 b   2 c   3 a

Headings
1 North America   2 Japan   3 Norway

Questions
1 Japan   2 Norway   3 North America, Japan
4 Norway   5 North America   6 Norway
7 North America and Norway   8 North America
9 North America and Japan   10 North America
11 Norway   12 Japan

Edinburgh – city of festivals

Read about Edinburgh's festivals and complete the captions under the photographs (1–4).

The Scottish city of Edinburgh has become famous for its arts festivals. Each year, there are eleven big festivals, including a book festival, a film festival, and a jazz and blues festival. Its two biggest festivals are the Edinburgh International Festival and the Edinburgh Fringe Festival. They both *take place* during August and last for three weeks. During this time, the city comes alive with music, drama and dance. Performances take place in theatres and concert halls. At the Fringe Festival, people perform in pubs, tents and even private rooms. There are street performers on every corner and there are thousands of visitors to the city every day.

The Edinburgh International Festival

The Edinburgh International Festival is a very *prestigious* festival and some of the world's best actors, dancers, musicians and singers come to the city to *take part*. The programme offers classical music by world-famous orchestras and opera singers. There are plays and performances by international theatre and dance companies. In past years, there have been performances by the Royal Philharmonic Orchestra, the National Theatre of Scotland, The State Ballet of Georgia and the African Children's Choir. Every year, more than 250,000 people buy tickets to see a concert or a play at the festival. On the last day of the festival, there is always a concert and a *spectacular* fireworks display in Edinburgh castle. The Scottish Chamber Orchestra plays music whilst the fireworks paint the sky in brilliant colours.

1

An .... performs at the Edinburgh .... Festival.

2

The ...., Jude Law, appeared at the Edinburgh .... Festival before he became a Hollywood film star.

The Edinburgh Fringe Festival

The Edinburgh Fringe Festival started in 1947 when eight theatre companies came to the Edinburgh Festival *unofficially*, that is without an invitation! They wanted to *attract* some of the crowds of people who were going to the 'official' festival to their own performances. Today, the *Fringe* Festival has become the biggest arts festival in the world. It offers theatre, comedy, dance, music, children's shows, musicals and exhibitions and is well known for its unusual and '*alternative*' artists and performances. Tickets for performances at the Fringe Festival are often cheaper than for the Edinburgh Festival and lots of street theatre is free. Anyone can take part in the festival, from Hollywood actors to drama clubs and student groups. A lot of the performances are different and exciting – and sometimes *shocking*. Each year, there are some *brilliant* performances at the Edinburgh Fringe Festival – and also some very bad ones! Many actors have become famous since performing at The Fringe Festival, including big names such as Hugh Grant, Robin Williams and Jude Law. In 2009, there were 1,300 performances a day.

Read about the festivals again, and then complete the table below with the correct information.

At which festival can you ...	The International Festival	The Fringe Festival
a see famous actors?		
b listen to opera?		
c laugh at some funny performers?		
d pay nothing to see a play?		
e see bad performances?		
f watch some fireworks?		
g see parents with young children?		
h go to a performance in a tent?		

3

During the month of ...., visitors from all over the world crowd the streets.

4

You can see .... everywhere during the festival.

Answers:
Captions
1 orchestra / International **2** actor / Fringe
3 August **4** (street) peformers

Table
The Edinburgh International Festival a b f
The Fringe Festival a c d e g h

UNIT 2 READING EXPLORER **99**

1

Most people have heard of vampire bats. You have probably seen films where Count Dracula turns into a vampire bat and bites the neck of his victim. However, Dracula's home is in Transylvania in Central Europe but in real life, vampire bats are found only in Central and South America. Vampire bats are about the size of a mouse but their small teeth are very *sharp*. They use them to make a tiny cut in an animal's skin. They do this while the animal is sleeping. The cut *bleeds* slowly and the bat drinks the blood one drop at a time. When it has drunk about two large *spoonfuls* of blood, it flies away. Its sleeping victim hasn't felt a thing. Blood is a good source of nutrition and it is easy to find. Vampire bats survive by drinking blood. This feeding habit is called *'haematophagy'*. There are many other kinds of *bloodsuckers*. In fact, these creatures are everywhere – there's probably one close to you right now!

2

Mosquitoes are well-known *bloodsuckers*. They live near water and come out at night. The female mosquito drinks blood to feed her eggs. She uses her **proboscis** to make a hole in the victim's skin. The proboscis has six *needles*. Some of them are like tiny knives, which she uses to make the cut bigger. Then she *sucks* the blood through a tube in the proboscis. The protein in the blood will help her eggs to grow. In many countries mosquitoes carry malaria, which is a killer disease.

3

Bedbugs are very small **mites** that live in people's houses. They like warm places near their victims and beds are ideal. When people are sleeping peacefully, the bedbugs come out to feed. They are not dangerous and do not carry disease, but a bedbug's bite can give you an *itchy* rash.

4

Ticks live in woods and long grass and jump onto animals or people as they walk past. The tick digs under the **host's** skin and stays there for many days. This unwanted guest feeds slowly on the host's blood. Tick bites can be dangerous because they carry diseases. The host may not know the tick is there. Ticks are easier to see on white, so hikers should wear white socks over their trousers.

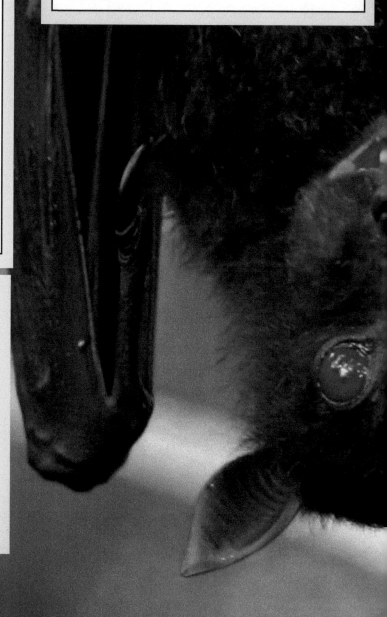

5

Leeches also attach themselves to their prey. They live in water and feed on fish or reptiles, but they like humans as well. They have two mouths and can drink more than twice their own weight. The leech makes a hole in its victim's skin with its proboscis. Then it sucks out the blood. When the leech has had enough, it *drops off* its victim. Doctors around the world have used leeches for centuries. They put them on a patient's skin to stop *swelling*. Leeches also make a chemical which stops **blood clots** and scientists are looking for ways to use this chemical to treat heart disease.

6

There are thousands of different creatures that drink blood. They include about 14,000 kinds of **arthropod,** as well as some *moths*. There are even birds that feed on blood, such as the oxpecker. This bird lives in Africa and preys on large animals, such as zebras and elephants. It uses its *beak* to **nibble** at *wounds* on an animal's skin.

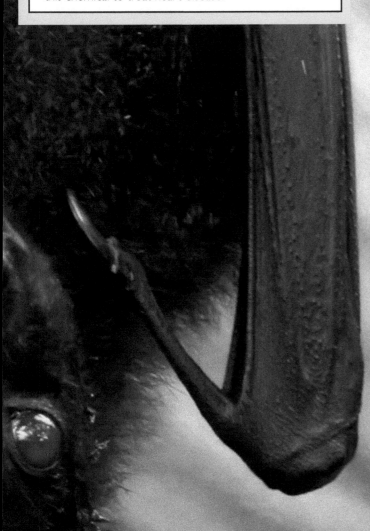

QUIZ: Vampire bats

1 Where do vampire bats live?
a in Eastern Europe
b in South and Central America
c in Africa and Asia

2 Why do they drink blood?
a Because they are thirsty.
b Because they need food.
c Because they are ill.

3 How big are vampire bats?
a as small as a mouse
b the same size as a large rat
c bigger than a mouse

4 How do vampire bats get blood from their prey?
a They bite their victim's neck.
b They cut a hole in an animal's skin.
c They suck blood from the injured animals.

5 How much blood does a vampire bat drink each time it feeds?
a one or two drops
b less than a spoonful
c more than a spoonful

Answers:
1b 2a 3e 4f 5c 6
d
Quiz
1b 2b 3a 4b 5c

Reading Explorer

Magical creatures

Read the text and complete the caption.

Amazon .... or .... seem orange when they are swimming in the waters of the Amazon river.

People in the Amazon tell folk stories about the 'botos' – magical creatures that live in the Amazon River. The creatures look orange when they are swimming in the water, but they are grey when they are out of the river. People believed that the botos could change into human beings. They came out of the water and *charmed* the local men and women, who followed them into the river and down to their underwater city.

The botos are, in fact, Amazon River dolphins. Although their skin is usually grey, some males are pink. This is probably caused by *scars*. The males are *aggressive* and are badly injured in fights. The pinkest males attract more females. However, when they are in the water, the dolphins seem to *glow* orange. This is because the vegetation and mud in the river is the colour of brown tea.

River dolphins look very different to *marine* dolphins. They have long, thin *beaks*, large *foreheads* and small *dorsal fins*. They also have shorter *flippers* and smaller eyes. In Amazon folk stories, the boto wears a hat to hide its strange-shaped head. Apart from the Amazonian boto, there are four other recognized species of river dolphin – the Ganges river and Indus river species, which are found in Asia, the Chinese river dolphin and the La Plata dolphin which lives in the salt water estuaries of Brazil and Argentina.

River dolphins are more at risk than *marine* dolphins because their habitat is more limited. They cannot swim away into the open sea like their marine cousins. In fact, they are on the list of the world's most endangered animals. There are fewer than 4,000 Indus and Ganges dolphins left in Asia. The Amazon and La Plata populations are healthier, but their numbers are still decreasing. This is because rivers have become more polluted and the dolphins are affected by the chemicals and waste in the water. In the Amazon, the rain forest is being cut down and commercial fish factories are being built. The fishermen take all the fish for the fish factories, so the dolphins have no food, and they are often killed accidentally in the fishing nets.

The story of the baiji, or Chinese river dolphin, shows how human activity can destroy a species. The Yangtze river was once home to a healthy population of river dolphins. However, the Yangtze is one of the most polluted rivers in the world. Its waters are *contaminated* by *toxic waste*, which also poisons the fish. As a result, the baiji's natural habitat has been destroyed. The last dolphin was seen in 2006 and experts today believe that the baiji is probably *extinct*. Even if one or two dolphins are found, it is not enough to save them.

Quiz: True or False?

	T	F
1 People in the Amazon believed the botos were magical creatures with special powers.	☐	☐
2 Botos have orange skin.	☐	☐
3 The males often have a lot of scars on their skin.	☐	☐
4 There were five species of river dolphin, but one of these is now probably extinct.	☐	☐
5 River dolphins can swim into the open sea to escape from polluted rivers.	☐	☐
6 Marine dolphins have longer flippers and larger eyes than river dolphins.	☐	☐
7 Amazon River dolphins are disappearing because they are hunted for food by local people.	☐	☐
8 The natural habitat of the Chinese river dolphins was destroyed by poisonous waste.	☐	☐
9 Nobody has seen a Chinese river dolphin since 2006.	☐	☐
10 There is still time to save the Chinese river dolphin.	☐	☐

Reading Explorer

The Amish

Read about the Amish and put a tick (✓) next to the sentences that are correct and a cross (✗) next to the incorrect sentences.

..... **1** The Amish are not allowed to drive cars.

..... **2** They work in factories and offices.

..... **3** Everyone has to follow the rules of the church.

..... **4** Small communities are not as strict as large communities.

..... **5** Amish parents are not open-minded.

..... **6** During Rumspringa, Amish teenagers don't have to help their parents at home.

..... **7** Girls are not allowed to wear trousers.

..... **8** Boys and girls can go out with each other when they are sixteen.

..... **9** During Rumspringa, teenagers can smoke and drink alcohol.

.....**10** If a young person decides to leave, they can never return.

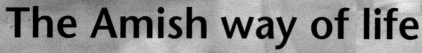

The Amish way of life

The Amish live in communities in North America. Their way of life is old-fashioned and simple. They do not have any electricity or modern machinery. They live without technology, so there are no computers and no television. They aren't allowed to travel in cars, so they ride in a *buggy* or walk. Most people work on farms and produce their own food. They have their own schools, but children leave school at the age of fourteen.

The Amish church has a lot of power in the *community*. It makes the rules which everybody has to follow. Smaller communities are usually stricter than larger ones. In big communities, like those in Pennsylvania and Ohio, the rules are more *relaxed*. The Amish sometimes *mix with* non-Amish people (who the Amish call 'English'). They can go into town or sell their fruit and vegetables at local markets. In small, strict communities, the Amish have no contact with the modern world. They aren't allowed to see an 'English' doctor or go to a modern hospital.

Amish teenagers

Amish parents are old-fashioned and strict, but their children look up to them. Young people have to wear traditional clothes and have simple, old-fashioned hairstyles. The girls have to wear long dresses or skirts, with an *apron* and a cap. The boys wear trousers, light-coloured shirts and a hat. The children play an active part in family life. The boys usually have to help their fathers on the family farm or with heavy work like *chopping firewood*. The girls help their mothers with the cooking and housework and are often responsible for looking after their younger brothers and sisters.

Amish teenagers are allowed to have friends of the opposite sex, but they cannot have boyfriends or girlfriends until they are sixteen. This is when '*Rumspringa*' begins. *Rumspringa* refers to *adolescence*, when young people are naturally more *rebellious*. When teenagers behave badly, the community is more open-minded and less strict. They let boys and girls go out with each other and many parents hope they will find a husband or wife.

In small communities, teenagers sometimes secretly smoke or drink alcohol, but it is difficult to break the rules without being seen. However, in large communities there is a *hidden* teenage culture. Some Amish teenagers meet up in groups and change their clothes and hairstyles. The girls wear jewellery and put on make-up. Then they go out into the nearest 'English' town where they sometimes mix with non-Amish teenagers. Sometimes they even drink alcohol and go out with 'English' boys and girls.

Rumspringa can last for a short time or until a person is twenty-five. At the end of *Rumspringa*, young people must choose the Amish way of life, or leave the community for ever. Most decide to stay and be *baptised* into the Amish church. Then they must obey all the rules and can only marry another member of church.

Boys and girls are allowed to be friends and have fun together.

An Amish girl from Pennsylvania rides in a buggy.

Answers:

1 ✓ 2 ✗ 3 ✓ 4 false 5 true 6 false
7 true 8 false 9 false 10 true

Reading Explorer

Nature's brilliant designs

Look at the photos and read the article. Match the photos (a–f) with the captions (1–7). There is one extra caption.

1 The thorny devil uses its foot to drink water.
2 Termites keep their nests cool even in the African jungle.
3 A baby lizard can stand with its feet in boiling water.
4 If a cocklebur sticks to your clothes, it won't be easy to take off.
5 The feet on the Stickybot will allow it to walk anywhere.
6 When you examine shark skin under a microscope you can see its scales.
7 The boxfish is the most aerodynamic fish in the ocean.

a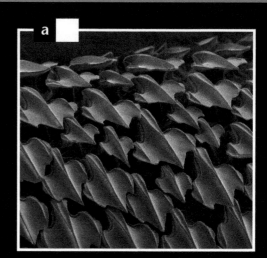

d

b

c

e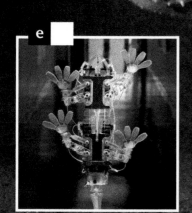

f

For many years, biologists, engineers and other scientists have used *designs* from plants and animals in order to solve problems in engineering, medicine and other fields. The scientific name for this is biomimetics. Back in 1948, a Swiss engineer, George de Mestral came home from a walk and found *cockleburs stuck* to his coat. He examined them carefully and discovered that their *spines* had tiny *hooks* on the end. He copied the design and invented Velcro. This is an early example of biomimetics.

More recent products include a bionic car and a swimsuit for Olympic swimmers. Engineers at Mercedes Benz based the design of their new *aerodynamic* car on the shape of the boxfish. This fish can swim six times the length of its body in one second. Speedo Fastskin allows swimmers to swim much faster than they could before. The special material is similar to sharkskin. It is made of *microscopic scales* which reduce *friction*.

Today, many scientists and

engineers are working on new biomimetic projects. In Japan, medical researchers are developing a new *hypodermic needle*. It has a *jagged edge*, just like a mosquito's proboscis. This means that *injections* will hurt less. In Zimbabwe, architects are studying *termites*. If they can understand how termites move the air around inside their *nests*, it will help them to build more *effective air-conditioning systems* for buildings. In America, teams of scientists are developing a robotic *gecko*, called the 'stickybot'. Geckos can climb up and down walls. They have millions of hairs on their toes, which stick to anything. The stickybot will work in the same way, and will be used in search and rescue operations.

English environmental biologist, Andrew Parker, has worked on a lot of biomimetics projects. His office is in the National History Museum in London, which has huge collections of animal *specimens* from all over the world. 'The museum is a *treasure chest* of brilliant design,' says Parker. 'I could look through here and find 50 biomimetics projects in half an hour.'

Parker has investigated the designs of many different species, especially birds and insects. However, his latest project involves a very special kind of lizard. The thorny devil is a very small lizard that lives in the Australian outback. It has sharp *thorns* all over its body and looks like a baby dinosaur. And it can perform an amazing trick. It stands on *damp* sand and drinks through its foot! Water from the sand collects on its feet, travels up its legs and along its back until it reaches the lizard's mouth. Parker has discovered that the lizard's skin has special scales which move the water along. With the help of engineers, he is working on a device to collect water in the desert. If the design is successful, it could save many lives.

a

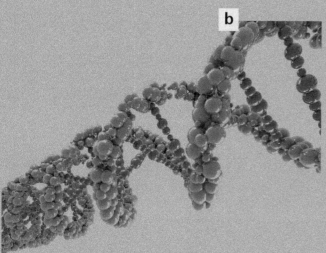
b

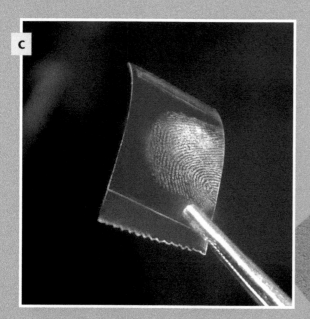
c

Crime scene investigator

At the crime scene

It is very early in the morning. You are a crime scene investigator. You have just arrived at the scene of a robbery in a sports shop. The thieves stole expensive sports equipment, money and bikes. There is a crowd of people outside the shop. The shop window is broken and there is glass on the ground. A detective comes over to you and asks you where you want to start. You tell her to put police *tape* across the area and to keep people away. Then you put on your plastic gloves. If you want to catch the criminal, you will need to find some evidence.

The photos show some of the evidence left by the thieves. Can you say what each piece of evidence is? Match the words (1–5) below with the pictures (a–e). Check your answers at the bottom of the page.

1 clear tape
2 DNA
3 fingerprint
4 footprint
5 tyre tracks

You decide to start outside. You talk to a man who says that he saw a man driving away from the scene. You ask a policeman to take him to the police station to give a witness statement. Then you look at the ground. You see *muddy* tyre tracks and footprints. First, you measure the distance between each footprint. If you can calculate how big the man's *footsteps* are, you will know how tall he is. Then you ask a police photographer to take a photo of the *footprint*. When you get back to the police station, you will be able to check the *pattern* on a database. If one of the patterns matches, you will know what kind of shoe the thief wears. Next, you look closely at the *tyre tracks* and find lots of clues.

What do these clues tell you? Write down your ideas, then read the paragraph below to check.

1 the pattern on the tyre tracks
2 seeds from a tree, stuck in the muddy tracks
3 cough sweets

That's right! You now know what type of car the thief was driving. You also know where he was before he robbed the shop because the *seeds* are from trees that only grow in warm coastal climates. If your calculations are right, the *suspect* has a cough and lives on the coast, about 200 kilometres south of the city.

Read about what happens and answer the questions in brackets in the text.

Next you go inside the shop. You look for fingerprints but, at first, you cannot find any. (*Why not?*) But, wait a moment. What's that on the floor? It's the paper from a cough sweet. You put white *powder* over the paper, and press clear *tape* onto it. Then you carefully lift up the tape and put it in a plastic bag. (*Why do you do this?*) Then you find a hair on the sweet *wrapper*. You think there might be some *saliva* on it too. You tell the detective to send them to the laboratory. (*What will the scientists in the lab do?*) You have now done everything you can and leave the crime scene.

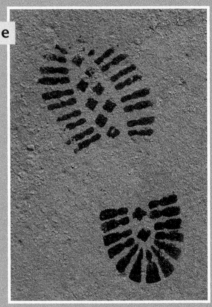

Complete the paragraph below.

At the police station

When you get back to the station, you will compare the ¹ .... to those on police files. If you find ones that match, you will know the ² .... of the suspect.

You must now wait for the lab results. If you are lucky, the ³ .... from the saliva will match a *profile* on the database. This means that you will have some very *solid* evidence. And you also know where to find your suspect!

Answers:

Photos
a fingerprints   b DNA   c clear tape   d tyre tracks   e footprint

Questions
The thief probably wore gloves.   There are fingerprints on the cough-sweet paper.   They will do tests on the saliva to get a DNA profile of the suspect.

At the police station
1 fingerprints   2 name   3 DNA

Reading Explorer

Be an eco-tourist

Complete the text with words in the box.

environment	foreign holidays
hotels	tents tourists

Would you like to go on a fantastic holiday and protect the planet at the same time? Eco-tours are a cool way to have fun on holiday and be green at the same time.

Although [1] .... are exciting, tourism can damage the environment. [2] .... are often careless and drop litter or damage the places they visit. They do not use *marked footpaths*, they pick wild flowers and sometimes disturb the wildlife. In poor countries, visitors usually stay in comfortable, modern [3] .... where they use up *limited* water and *fuel*.

Eco-tourists are more knowledgeable about the [4] .... than ordinary tourists. They follow one golden rule: take only photographs, leave only footprints. They enjoy travelling to natural areas to observe wild animals and plants and prefer staying in *log cabins* or [5] .... An eco-tourist would never book him or herself into four-star accomodation. Eco-tourists also explore local cultures and help with conservation projects.

Read about five eco-holidays and match the holidays (1–5) with the destinations.

India ☐

Belize ☐

Japan ☐

Peru ☐

Sweden ☐

1

THE HOLIDAY: Look for bottlenose dolphins and *manatees* as you sail around tropical islands. Dolphins are friendly and *inquisitive*, so it won't be long before they come to have a look at you. However, make sure you don't forget to count how many there are. When you need a break, dive into the crystal blue waters of the Caribbean. If you love dolphins, this is the holiday for you!

WHY IT'S ECO-FRIENDLY: Counting dolphins and manatees helps scientists find out if the animal's habitat is *thriving*.

2

THE HOLIDAY: Travel to the grasslands at the base the beautiful Mount Fuji and catch endangered Reverdin's blue butterflies. If you catch one, you should carefully mark an identification number on its wing before you let it fly away again. If you want a day off, you could go for a hike in the hills around the mountain. Or you could just relax in your traditional house.

WHY IT'S ECO-FRIENDLY: The marks on the butterflies' wings allow scientists to monitor the Reverdin's population and its natural habitat.

3

THE HOLIDAY: Go on safari in the Ranthambore National Park. The park is home to endangered Bengal tigers as well as leopards and other wild animals. Here in the park, the tigers are protected from hunters and their wild habitat is preserved. While you are there, you can also visit the Taj Mahal and other historic buildings – but remember to take off your shoes before you enter a temple.

WHY IT'S ECO-FRIENDLY: Your entrance fee helps tiger conservation.

4

THE HOLIDAY: Go *reindeer* trekking with the native Sami people. As you trek across the Arctic, the reindeer will carry your rucksack for you and your Sami guide will tell you all about the Sami way of life. The Sami have survived for many years by *herding* reindeer across Scandinavia and Russia. You will live with the Sami, eat local food and sleep in a tent called a 'kata'.

WHY IT'S ECO-FRIENDLY: The native land of the Sami is threatened because many trees have been cut down. If you support the Sami, you can help them conserve their way of life.

5

THE HOLIDAY: Visit the Amazon and look down on the rainforest from the 115-foot high walkway. As you walk along near the tops of the trees, you will enjoy spectacular views. Take a boat down the Amazon river and you will see pink dolphins swimming in the water. Your accommodation will be at the ExplorNapo eco-lodge. There's no electricity here, but you will catch your own *piranha* fish for dinner and sleep in a room made from *palm* leaves.

WHY IT'S ECO-FRIENDLY: The lodge conserves natural resources and gives money to saving the rainforest.

Which holiday(s) would you choose if you:

a wanted to learn about another culture?

....

b liked sailing?

....

c enjoyed adventure holidays?

....

d loved nature and walking holidays?

....

e were interested in helping endangered species?

....

f liked sightseeing?

....

g wanted to swim with dolphins?

....

Answers:

Text
1 foreign holidays   **2** tourists   **3** hotels
4 environment   **5** tents

Destinations
1 Belize   **2** Japan   **3** India   **4** Sweden   **5** Peru

Holidays
a Sweden   **b** Belize   **c** Peru, Sweden   **d** Japan
e India, Belize, Japan   **f** India,   **g** Belize